PALESTINE:

CHRONICLE OF A PLANNED TRAGEDY

By

Kassem Asmar Castellanos

CONTENT

Pág.

INTRODUCTION   5

1. GENERAL EXPLANATION OF THE CONFLICT   9

THE BEGINNING OF THE PALESTINIAN PROBLEM   9

THE ZIONIST ARGUMENT OF A HISTORIC LEGACY ACCORDING TO A   14
" DIVINE MANDATE"

THE FORMAL BEGINNNIG OF THE JEWISH MIGRATIONS AND THE BALFOUR   18
DECLARATION

PALESTINE AND THE POST- WORLD WAR II STAGE   21

CONSEQUENCES OF THE ARAB-ISRAELI WAR OF 1948   26

AL NAKBA; THE PALESTINIAN CATASTROPHE SPREADS OUT   29

THE ZIONIST PLAN DALET   32

THE ZIONIST ATTEMPT TO HIDE THEIR CRIMES   34

MOODS ARE EXACERBATED   39

2. THE ISRAELI EXPANSIONISM, AS AN EXCUSE TO CONTROL THE WATER   44
RESOURCES AND THE THEFT OF LANDS

3. JEWISH SETTLEMENTS IN THE OCCUPIED TERRITORIES, THE MOST   54
DIFFICULT OBSTACLE TO REACH A PEACE AGREEMENT

4. ISRAEL AND PALESTINE FROM THE ANALYTICAL VIEWPOINT OF THE   71
MOST DISTINGUISHED REVISIONISTS

5. THE SEPARATION WALL; A STRATEGY THAT GOES BEYOND THE ISSUE   90
OF SECURITY

6. THE GAZA STRIP, LIVING WITH THE SIEGE AND THE ISRAELI BLOCKADE   97

7. THE PALESTINIANS IN NABLUS, HEBRON, BETHLEHEM, QALQILYA, JENIN   109
AND JERUSALEM, UNDER THE OCCUPATION FORCES

8. THE JEWISH'S LOBBY AND THE UNITED NATIONS IN THE ISRAELI-   131
PALESTINIAN CONFLICT

9. PALESTINIAN-ISRAELI PEACE PROCESS: MORE THAN TWENTY YEARS OF   136
DIALOGUE WITHOUT ANY IMPORTANT PROGRESS

BIBLIOGRAPHY   152

INTRODUCTION

Usually, we hear from different sectors of society coincidental opinions in the sense of complexity to understand the conflict of the Middle East and more specifically the Palestinian-Israeli conflict. Well, the main reason of this book is to expose in the clearest way the conflict that for many years and decades, has involved Arabs and Israelis and specifically Palestinians, from a wide perspective but at the same time very succinct, in such a way that it covers different contemporary history fields, expecting that most significant details of that problem, being kept in mind with such clarity, that the understanding of its different contents should be easy.

The semantic style used in the writing of this book is simple, in order to be accessible for any sector of society, and it was kept in mind the most important facts that should not be omitted from the author's viewpoint, and the chronological order that explains the different conflicting processes of the Palestinian problem, prove that there wasn't improvisation of any kind, due to the seriousness of the research that the author had in mind in each topic contained in this book.

I have the pleasure to offer to the international community, regardless of the cultural and educational level of the reader, my book titled "Palestine: Chronicle of a Planned Tragedy", in which the conflict is narrated from its start in 1897, when was carried out the first Zionist world congress led by Theodor Herzl where it devised the first conspiracy lines against the Palestinians, whose aim has been always to seize every corner of the Palestinian territory, until the most recently dates that show a series of summits, meeting and dialogues of peace between Palestinians and Israelis that have ended in big failures.

With the spirit to avoid mistrusts and doubt about the contents of this book, I invite you to test each paragraph of this interesting work, contrasting it with the innumerable resources that exist for the topic mentioned and that are available for each reader, therefore, I reiterate to postpone any critical towards me, without having made any study and serious analysis about this topic.

Kassem Asmar Castellanos   *July, 2,014*

By Kassem Asmar Castellanos

1. GENERAL EXPLANATION OF THE CONFLICT

THE BEGINNING OF THE PALESTINIAN PROBLEM

The problems in the Middle East involve several Arabian countries including Israel although in particular Palestinians and Syrians for being at this moment directly linked to the conflict. From its beginning, the Palestinians and the Jews were the main figures of what would be one of the most antagonistic episodes in the contemporary age that started at the end of 19th century and its prolongation continues well into the 21th century, having as witnesses the different generational descendants that under the protection of hope, do not lose the faith of being able to shout out someday "at last, Palestine is free from all occupation".

There are many questions that surround the Palestinian-Israeli problem, but the inescapable question that many different societies formulate is the following; How did the Palestinian-Israeli conflict start? To answer that question we are obligated to make a retrospective glance to analyze the events at the end of the 19th century that allow us to understand the reasons and causes of its beginning.

The late 19th century, an ideological movement with religious-nationalistic tendency had risen in Europe, whose main vision was concentrated in conceiving an ambitious project whose purpose was to create a State for the Jews that lived in many different places throughout the world, especially in Europe. This movement was known as Zionism. Though in the beginning, Zionism was introduced as a political movement but this aspect was questioned due to the predominate religious elements in its ideology.

After a series of meetings of different Zionist leaders, among them was their maximum representative, the Hungarian Theodor Herzl who decided that the best place to establish a homeland for the Jewish community was Palestine, thanks to an elemental reason that they had considered, that the origin of the Jewish religion was rooted on this land. From then on, there was no doubt that the base of the Zionism project was eminently religious with a "special comprehension".

By Kassem Asmar Castellanos

Even nowadays, many analysts and people don't doubt in describing the state of Israel as racist because of the Zionist program gives Israeli nationality to all of those who practices the Jewish religion and that, confirms the fact that the Zionist movement is based on religious dogma, more than any other ideological rule. On the other hand, it is not difficult to conclude that the Zionist movement by its different tendencies, is a fanatic movement.

Though, long before the first Zionist meeting that Theodor Herzl organized, there had already been dialogues about a homeland for Jewish in Palestine, but who gave it worldwide acceptance as a Zionist organization in a proper sense was Herzl in 1897 when he called for a great congress meeting of the Zionist currents from different places and from then on, they started talking about the world Zionist organization.

It should be noted that a decade before the first congress; they had already materialized the idea with the first Jewish emigrations to Palestine but in a smaller scale though. But the claims of the world Zionist movement went beyond of the intrinsic idea of creating a home or state for the Jewish in Palestine. In their objectives, the firm confidence was always latent that the nationalist project should embrace the whole of Palestine because from the perspective of the Zionist interpretation of the scriptures "so should be". Although according to the Zionist ideology, the ancient residents who were Arab-Palestinians, Should be thrown out, too.

What was the first point that according to the global aims of the world Zionist movement at the end of the 19th century that should be carry out? To initiate and regulate continuous Jewish migrations from different parts of Europe to Palestine and that task was always accompanied by great caution and cunning to not raise suspicion in the Arab population in Palestine, because the Zionists were selling the idea that they were emigrants whose purpose was not going beyond of working on agricultural issues.

Obviously, this task was difficult, keeping in mind the almost total absence of Jewish inhabitants in the area and particularly in Palestine. At the end of the 19th century, the total of the Palestinian population was 460.000 people, of those, 5% were

By Kassem Asmar Castellanos

Jewish and the rest, Arab-Palestinians.

In those days, the entire region was under domain of the Ottoman Empire (currently Turkey) that had been there for several centuries. Nonetheless, all people who lived in Palestine, which were formed mainly by Arab-Palestinians, and in much fewer numbers by Jews. It is important to explain that the Ottomans had taken control of Syria, Lebanon, Jordan, Iraq and part of Egypt, although, it is relevant to point out that the geographical map of Palestine in the time that the Ottoman Empire had the control of this region, was different to what we call Palestine now, because in those days it was formed by a part of Syria, Lebanon and Jordan. That region was known as the Great Syrian Provence.

It is also imperative to underline that Christians, Jews, and Muslims co-existed without inconvenient in the region, until the world Zionist organization formalized its purpose fraught with extreme evil. From then, the course of history in the Middle East changed forever.

The Arab-Palestinians coming from the name "Fillisters" have always been throughout centuries in that region, known as Palestine, but unfortunately remains only 22% of Palestine, after the continuous Zionist theft, with the alliance and assistance of the British and American that contributed to change the Palestinian geographical map, with the theft of 78% of Palestine until the beginning of 1948 and with a particular cynicism of showing their aim of taking over of the last square meter of Palestine as it actually occurred. But, who are the Palestinians? Unlike what most of Jews say, who want to invert the equation, referring to the Palestinians as people without history and culture, a lie and extraordinary fraud as one of the Zionist tactics, but keeping in mind that Israel has an ambition of taking full control of Palestine and after all, disqualifying the culture and origin of the Palestinian people, this gives us the true dimension of the Zionist aims of re-editing history with deceptions to justify their criminal intentions against the Palestinian people, as it appears in the records of the Zionist organization, led by Theodor Herzl and Ben Gurion.

By Kassem Asmar Castellanos

Palestinians settled in this region for many centuries and by obvious reasons, adopted different religions and beliefs consistent with the periods of conquests, but in no case we can say it is not a people with an rooted origin, although adopted different religions including the Jewish and Christian religion and at the time of the rise of Islam, with the Arabic ruling in the region in the 7th century, Palestinians definitively adopted the religion of Islam or Muslim.

Since centuries they were called Arab-Palestinians to make the distinction of culture and language, however it is also true that there are many Christians, among them a very famous population which is Bethlehem, where its inhabitants are eminently Christians, then what makes that a claim is valid at the moment of pretending to defend the rights of a people over a specific territory? Obviously its continuous link over the land that corroborates that they have had roots there throughout centuries, in addition to appreciate and identify a culture and a language perfectly distinguishable and therefore, Palestinians fulfill with all civilized rules of the international legal order that goes against the Machiavellian pact devised by the Zionist leaders to take absolute control of Palestine with the pathetic argument that simply they are fulfilling a "Divine Mandate".

One of the most painful betrayals comes precisely from those who being well received and welcomed into the bosom of a home; but the host can end receiving a stab in the back as a signal of "gratitude". This is what precisely happened with the Palestinians when they received, peacefully, the early migrations of the Jews in Palestine, because the main argument was, that they needed to work on agricultural labors, to which the Palestinians did not oppose to, but entering the 20th century, the facts showed a panorama completely different, because there was more and more hints and evidences what it was brewing went far beyond the simple intention of planting tomatoes and potatoes, because the tentacles of Zionism gave their first whips at the beginning, in an efficient way, to seize the first territorial portions with the blessing of the newly arrived British, forcing indignant Palestinians to show their first reactions and dispute as expression of resistance towards the incipient Zionist expansionism but in terms of results, the balance was tilted in

By Kassem Asmar Castellanos

favor of the Zionists because they had been receiving military supplies by the British, which remained as a constant to the end of the conflagration of World War II.

By Kassem Asmar Castellanos

THE ZIONIST ARGUMENT OF A HISTORIC LEGACY ACCORDING TO A "DIVINE MANDATE"

Zionism has as main representative and creator, the Hungarian Theodor Herzl, that Unlike most contemporary Jews where intend to justify the creation of a Jewish State in Palestine by issues of a "Divine Mandate" and the continuous persecutions of the Jewish people throughout history, Herzl adds something that goes beyond these assumptions, because his concern was to separate them from those who were not Jews, through the assignment of a homeland exclusively for the Jews and obviously could not be an exception without mentioning the famous "Divine Mandate". This confirms that the highest representative of Zionism was conscious that the problem at the end of the 19th century and the start of 20th was not a question of Jewish persecutions, except counted facts.

What happened in the Second World War with the insanity acts of the Nazi regime, should not be considered as something widespread against the Jewish people due to that feeling of hate belonged to a group of henchmen of the Nazi regime, with total absence of sensitivity where human massacres were circumscribed as statistical aspects, however we must not forget that this same insane regime killed more than 16 million Russians and this is not an intent of minimizing the apocalyptic situation which the Jewish people suffered by the Holocaust of the last World War in the hands of the Nazi regime. It seeks to emphasize that it should not justify the unjustifiable, from the terrible events of the Holocaust and trying to convert that event as a valid framework and show it as a chase on a large scale from different horizons against the Jewish people, that forced them to find as solution a homeland in Palestine with the approval of the contents in the old testament. This is proved when Theodor Herzl said: "the solution of the Jewish issue was not to fight to end anti-Semitism and achieve total equality of the Jews in countries where they lived, but to separate the Jewish from those who were not ..."

From the above we can conclude that the same arguments and contents of the world Zionist movement, explain with clear neatness that the question of establishing a homeland in Palestine at the expense of the Arab-Palestinians, was a matter that went far beyond the daily experiences that Jews had in the countries where they were originally.

All of this leads us to a path which content shows that the fundamental reason to create a Jewish State in Palestine it is not related to the persecutions of the Jews in ancient times, but the primordial 'justification' is in the fact that the Zionist movement seeks to sentence at an angle purely religious, where Palestine is for Jews by "Divine Mandate" and therefore the only ones who have the right to live in Palestine are those that profess the Jewish religion. In others words, a recent convert Jew that professes the Jewish religion, has more right to live in Palestine than a Palestinian who has ancestral roots of many centuries. Obviously, that gives us the right to think that the Zionist manifest was drafted with an aim clearly racist and sectarian by emphasizing the supremacy of the Jewish race, trampling on the rights of the Palestinian people. So, on the basis of that order of concepts, Zionism more than a political movement is a movement radically religious and racist. Mahatma Gandhi said in late 1938: "Palestine belongs to the Arabs in the same sense that England belongs to the English for France to the French ". "It is wrong and inhuman to impose the Jews to the Arabs and there is no doubt that it would be a crime against humanity, to humiliate the proud Arab inhabitants of Palestine so that the Jews could restore partly or completely their national home".

"My sympathy does not blind me to the requirements of Justice. The cry for the national home for the Jews does not make much appeal for me. Rely on the Bible to request with tenacity their return to Palestine, but the Bible is the first stage of their religion that has passed through many others, such as Christian or Buddhist religions. Why should they not like other people of the earth, make that country their home where they are born and where they earn their livelihood?"

Zionism has taken advantage the theme of religion to make apology with all forms of injustice and illegal acts against the Palestinians in order to retain their lands. Never before, a group of fanatics had used religion with so much vehemence to cause so much damage and wickedness as the World Zionist movement and the State of Israel have done against the Palestinian people and this has been going on for more than 110 years since this pernicious plan was put into operation at the end of the19th century.

It is clearly proved that Israel has raised its basis, manipulating its own Jewish history, trying to support a worn out thesis with ephemeral Fundamentals so irrational that it ends up falling down by the weight of its own lies. As well as Muslim and Christian beliefs are religions and not a nationality, the same thing should happen with the Jewish religion. Then, the Zionist movements present the Jewish faith not as a religion but as a nationality, in order to justify the assault committed on the Palestinian territories through the endless migration of Jews to Palestine.

In conclusion, it is a huge farce that the Judaism should be looked at from a different viewpoint to what it is, i.e. a religion. So, no society that follows a particular faith, can take the contents of the scriptures of its religion as excuse, to commit abuses and injustices against other people with the pathetic argument that they are following a "Divine Mandate", and if it wasn't enough this deception, add another "justification" to its insidious project with this sad famous phrase "a land without people for a people without land", trying to show that Palestine was practically an uninhabited territory when the Jews began to arrive there. Obviously, this trickery could not last in the historical records, much less change the authentic records of history.

The Resolution 3379 of the General Assembly of the United Nations, had adopted in late 1975 a pronouncement as sentence against the Zionist acts, considering them as racist, but before constant pressure from Jewish organizations and President Bush himself, that Resolution was revoked 16 years later, i.e. in 1991. The circumstances that surrounded this revocation, to the astonishment of everyone, with a high content of blackmail and insolence, began at the end of 1991, when the Soviet Union and the United States, with the support of Spain, had convoked a peace conference for the Middle East, known as the Madrid Peace Conference. Israel put as a condition for its attendance that the Resolution 3379 about Zionism should be revoked and that happened.

By Kassem Asmar Castellanos

Returning to the topic, Herzl organized in Switzerland in 1897 the first Zionist Congress. To achieve his mission, sought support from Great Britain to help in the Foundation and creation of a homeland for the Jews in Palestine. For Such proposal, the British made an offer of a territory in somewhere uninhabited in Uganda but the Zionists said that it should be in Palestine.

By *Kassem Asmar Castellanos*

THE FORMAL BEGINNING OF THE JEWISH MIGRATIONS AND THE BALFOUR DECLARATION

After the Russian revolution, many Jews were persecuted and Zionism exploited this situation, convincing them to go to Palestine. These and other migrations from other places helped to increase constantly the number of Jews in Palestine. At Mid 1914 there were approximately 90,000 Jews in Palestine and everything indicated that the increase was incessant. The pressure of the Zionist movements in Europe gave its result, since reached to promote and bring forward an initiative known as the Balfour Declaration, making allusion to its creator Arthur Balfour, who without any kind of doubt or hesitation and with an imperialist language, had said that Great Britain supported the idea of creating a Jewish nation in Palestine. As soon as the English politician gave this "magical speech", many Jews continued arriving to Palestine and not strictly for tourism issues but for stealing the lands of Palestinians. A few years later, when the Arab- Palestinians realized the dimension of the outrage, started to protest but all pointed out that the Zionist process of taking over of Palestine looked like a locomotive without brakes and the Palestinian fate was dark.

The question is, How Great Britain became involved in Palestine? According to the condition of the Arabs in that region of the Middle East under the rule of the Ottoman Empire for four centuries, the idea of territories with independence was sounding better into the mind of their leaders. This new perspective of the region was exploited by the British who spared no efforts to propose an alliance to face in an armed conflict the Ottomans, in return, the British promised that once the Ottomans were defeated, they would compromise themselves to work in favor of the independence of different regions or territories. But in reality, the English had other plans because they had made that promise to the Arabs with the simple and transcendent reason to get the necessary support to ensure their presence in the region. With this tactic, the British had shown others ambitions embodied within the imperialistic British minds that didn't have the slightest relation with the Arab independence aspirations. It is prudent to point out that during the confrontation against the Ottoman Empire, at the same time there was a secret deal between Great Britain and

By Kassem Asmar Castellanos

France that established a commitment to share the Middle East, as if it was a real party. Once defeated the Ottoman Empire, the distribution would be done in the following way: France would stay with what today it is known as the Lebanon and Syria and part of Iraq and the British would be making presence and influence in great part of Iraq, Iran and what is now known as Palestine.

What at the beginning was for those people a special enthusiasm when believed the promises of the British, it ended up being a great disappointment and deception because the Arabs realized as soon as the English had defeated the Ottomans, that they were deceived. Therefore the metamorphosis of the Arabs' mood of the region was total because of the deception of the British was enormous. The Arabs went from a situation of considerable rejoicing to a state of disappointment and absolute discouragement.

If with the previous deceptive maneuvers was not enough, the English who already had a "right" to manage the zone according to their imperialist viewpoint, without much consultation with those nearby or distant, came to the conclusion that it wasn't so difficult to tell the Jews that they could establish a homeland in Palestine, because of the British government had shown so much generosity toward the Zionists. The English representative Arthur Balfour with a cynical language, included the phrase with a marked tone full of derision towards Arabs, said without hesitation, a Home for the Jews in Palestine meant that "there should be no prejudice to the Civil and religious rights toward other communities in Palestine", so comprehensive, right? But let's clarify that not only the permission that the English received to enter the region was noxious, because there was a big blunder committed by the Ottomans, allying with the German side during the first world war and that gave the perfect excuse to the English, under the pretext of the legitimate right to attack them, therefore they consolidated its presence in the region, just as it was proved after the end of the first World War.

By Kassem Asmar Castellanos

The Balfour Declaration, which was understood that it came from the first world power, was considered a real humiliation for the Arabs in the region and particularly for the Arab-Palestinians. In fact, this statement became green light for the arrival without interruption of more Jews to Palestine, thus already in 1928 it was estimated at 150,000 Jews established in Palestine.

With the rise of Adolfo Hitler in power, massively increased the Jewish migrations to Palestine, but also weapon smuggling was to the order of the day to arm the Jewish population, in order to reinforce its presence in Palestine and obviously to expand their presence in everywhere as the Zionists had planned it. The view was painted in the following manner; the balance of forces was leaning in favor of the Jews and their radical violent groups that began to create terror in many places of Palestine therefore was increasing the confrontations between Arabs and Jews.

The British giving displays of concern and with clear evidences of the true intentions of the Zionists to exert control over Palestine, the British authorities were furious and cancelled the Balfour Declaration but in practice, did it have any sense after having entered in functioning for more than 20 years?

Anyway, those Jews who were living in Palestine interpreted that English threat as a possible alliance with the Arabs and they began to attack the British positions. The most famous and remembered was that they perpetrated against the barracks of British officers whose installation was in the well- known hotel King David in Jerusalem where the terrorist gangs of Menachem Begin, placed explosives and blew up part of the hotel. The outcome was 90 dead and the political authorities in London understood that the situation was out of control and sent the problem that they themselves had created, to the United Nations in 1947.

If the Zionist movement could strengthen its Machiavellian plan to seize Palestine thanks to the participation of Great Britain, which came after the second World War, continued sinking more into misfortune the Arabs, and particularly the Palestinians, with the support of other more powerful imperialist nation, for the expansionism and criminal cause of the Zionist movement, this empire is called the United States of America.

By Kassem Asmar Castellanos

PALESTINE AND THE POST-WORLD WAR II STAGE

Due to the successive Jewish migrations from Europe to Palestine, these increased considerably to reach one-third of the total population resident in Palestine, but remained much smaller in comparison with the Arab-Palestinians that were more than 65% of the total population, also the Palestinians remained being the owners of the majority of the land in Palestine, despite the territorial plunder. It is imperative to remember that at the beginning of the 20th Century the Palestinian population controlled 90% of the land in Palestine while the Jewish population was hardly approaching 10%. However, in 1947 the General Assembly of the UN and in an abusive way with evident favoring to the Jewish aspirations, resolved to give them 56% of the Palestinian territory at a stroke, this fact exacerbated the patience of all Arabs in the region that without thinking twice, they rejected such nonsense. The tension increased and immediately after Ben Gurion read out the speech about declaration of independence of Israel, troops from Syria, Egypt and Iraq attacked the newly created State of Israel. The start of the first war between Arabs and Israelis was a reality, as also the Zionist warlike supremacy, moreover they were preparing for that kind of eventualities with weapons much more sophisticated than that the Arabs had although were considerably greater in numbers, could not go against a more organized army in preparation and in armament.

But returning to highlight the real Zionist aspirations on Palestine where they intend with some understatement to justify its increasingly less credible historic allegation, that all they want is comply with a "stipulated requirement" given by the Scriptures of the old testament where supposedly, gives power and right to the Jewish people with the well-known "Divine Mandate" of committing an assault on the Palestinian territory. They go beyond when the Zionist organizations certify with handwriting that they cannot escape of natural and historical right that corresponds to them and that is the return to their land "the promised land", after having been expelled by the Romans at the beginning of the Christian era. The historical fact that they are trying to hide is that the few Jews who remained, most of them accepted the Christian religion and then when the messengers of the current Muslim arrived in

By Kassem Asmar Castellanos

most of the regions of the Middle East including Palestine, in the seventh century, many Jews and Christians adopted this new religious faith in Palestine and this openly contradict the Zionist claims about this land in the sense that they found it uninhabited when they began to arrive in the late 19th century and early of the 20th. The Jews acknowledge that they were absent for almost 2000 years since they were expelled from Palestine by the Roman Empire, is it not evidence that the Palestinians had constant presence during centuries in Palestine? Historic and natural rights that alleges and claims the Jewish people, Is it more transcendent than the countless generations of Palestinians who had established their roots and links with their lands for several centuries? This would be equivalent to say with daring that France, in its inception as colonizer country in Algeria, had found a land uninhabited, knowing that in 1830 there were over two million Algerians in this part of the North of Africa

Obviously that the teachings of the early Zionists with their descendants, had the purpose of redesigning and rewrite the Palestinian history to justify and legalize their assault that culminated with the mega project of the theft of Palestine, with the poor argument that those lands were abandoned at the start of the 20th century and the few, but very few Arabs who were in the area, were in backwardness conditions so obvious that it could compare with the style of the primitive people and, in these circumstances, the intentions of the Jews was to bring progress and welfare to the Palestinian "uninhabited" land. The Zionists tried to preserve as well as was possible their monumental lie but in the 21st century with the developments and the technological culture within the reach of everyone, this brief Zionist exposure about Palestine is not virtually credible by anyone except those few Zionists that with their ideologies, don´t benefit a sincere and peaceful coexistence among people.

The Zionists, in isolation, could not have done a project of such dimension without the participation of powers as was evidenced with the political and military support of the British and Americans from the epilogue of 1947. This last one has kept his support fraternizing their relationships with the Zionist State in all levels and areas but especially, providing exorbitant financial and military aid, as well as making the Israeli State as an untouchable country

By Kassem Asmar Castellanos

with the broad support of American foreign policy, that doesn't save any effort to stop any legal action by the international community that pretends to stop the actions of Israeli expansionism.

At that time, the requirement for an initiative would be feasible in the General Assembly of the UN, had to have the support of two-thirds of delegations' votes of the countries. Seeing the United States that such support was not guaranteed, they devised the tactic that until today has been used, the pressure and threat. Of these pressures not even France could escape. But the great trap orchestrated by the Zionist movements and with the unconditional American support, began to take shape at the United Nations with the most blatant manner possible because the General Assembly had already approved the Resolution 106 which created a Special Commission in May 1947, in order to present a report as objective as possible to the General Assembly of the UN in order to prepare the stage for knowing how should be the partition of Palestine. The results of the investigation of the Commission were conclusive when said that the demographic configuration in Palestine was represented by 65% of Arab-Palestinians who totaled approximately 1.220.000 Palestinians and the Jews population was 33% who amounted approximately 600,000 inhabitants. That Commission left a note, explaining that in most of the areas of Palestine the Arab-Palestinians were majority. On the other hand, the Arabs were owners of 90% of the lands, while the Jews didn't have more than 10% of the lands. In synthesis, the recommendation of that Commission to the surprise of many was that it had to make a partition where 56% of Palestine should be for the Jews. The argument that showed this Commission is that several countries had made a commitment of establishing a home for the Jews in Palestine. This decision, clearly alarmed the Arabs therefore, rejected strongly this proposal, considering it completely inequitable.

After that report, a Special Committee was appointed in order to expand its study on the Palestine issue and they came to the conclusion that the UN did not have authority to make a partition in order to oblige a majority, which in this case were the Arab-Palestinians, to withdraw from a large portion of their territory for the benefit of a minority which in this case were the Jews. This

By Kassem Asmar Castellanos

conclusion and recommendation was ignored, especially by the power of American political maneuverability in the General Assembly of the United Nations, where the Resolution 181 finally was passed in a very misleading way at the end of November 1947. The Zionists had enough reasons to jump for joy, because the blow was brutal against the Palestinian people and the founder of Zionism Theodor Herzl with his turbid and lethal plan had left a dark stain on the sad record of humanity, but this blow was not definitive since the Palestinian people had to live others very difficult situation with many calamities thanks to the Zionist perspective of a so-called "Divine Mandate". It is not the first time that many injustices and acts of barbarism against humanity have been committed in the name of Holy Scriptures.

But returning to the aspect of the vote on the Resolution 181 of 1947 that was plagued with blackmailer maneuvers, moreover pressures and traps. Mrs. Tzipi Livni, who served as Minister of Foreign Affairs of Israel between 2006 and 2009 said that if the vote on the Resolution 181 was today, it would not have chance to be approved, judge yourself and draw your own conclusion.

What we have to highlight is that the powerful countries of the post-war led by the United States handled the vote at their own will, taking advantage of the countries economically subordinated to the North American imperialist market and with a certain financial aid, then the American task was not difficult because they manipulated the chess board without having any opponent and the result was plagued with injustices, therefore in a blink of an eye, the Palestinians had lost 56 % of their territory.

Since the creation of the United Nations, the State founded by the most illegitimate way was Israel but the topic doesn't stop there, because in order to stop the Israeli atrocities, dozens of Resolutions could not have important effects by the permanent use of the American veto that have protected and applauded the spiral of injustices committed against the Palestinian people.

Herzel wanted to give a political character to the World Zionist movement in 1897, at the Congress which he organized in Basel (Switzerland) in that same year with the aim of winning alliances of powerful countries as Great Britain, France and the United States but not only limited to search support of these countries, but also the private sectors of special vigor in the financial and media field, were also in their plans.

The Rothschild dynasty of German Jewish origin is a well-known family in the entire Western Europe by their wide foray on a large scale the financial business. That family started the business almost from scratch in the middle of the 18th century in Germany and at the beginning of the 19th century they had another headquarters in England and later in France, shortly after ranged in Vienna and Naples. In the mid-19th century the Rothschild dynasty was very famous throughout Europe for its activity related with the services offered by their banks. Their relationship with the Palestinian conflict began to take place at the end of the 19th century when Edmond Rothschild came to Palestine, which was under the control of the Ottoman Empire and then started to support "the Zionist cause" with great financial support for the creation of Jewish settlements as a stimulus to Jewish migration to Palestine.

The enormous contributions of the Rothschild family to the Zionist organizations and the State of Israel have remained up to today's date. This dynasty acquired such power and so much influence within the structure of the World Zionist movement, which the Israel Parliament known as the Knesset, the Supreme Court of Justice and the Supreme Court of Israel were built, with the money of the Rothschild's.

By Kassem Asmar Castellanos

CONSEQUENCES OF THE ARAB-ISRAELI WAR OF 1948

It is very probable that if the partition of Palestine had been made in a more equitable and fair way, the history would have been different because having assigned the largest part of the Palestinian territory to a minority who were Jews, this fact extolled the spirits of the Arab population in the region, moreover, the role of world imperialism headed by the United States had played a role of abuse of authority as a powerful nation, due to it should not be forgotten that Europe just began to rise from the devastation of the second World War and the United States had extended its hands over the old continent through the Marshall's plan for its reconstruction, needless to say of the countries of the Latin American region that were handled as puppets by the power of the North, so the stage was too easy in the main precinct of the General Assembly of the UN, therefore the United States directed the Orchestra with the will of their wishes and of the Zionists. The fate of the Arab-Palestinians was virtually sealed and they only had to wait for the respective performances of a shameful spectacle, trying to convince them that everything, it was doing in the most immaculate way but the results, in advance, were clearly known. On the other hand, the Arabs who were feeling greatly humiliated, adopted a position of rejection against the Resolution 181.

As soon as was created the Jewish State known as Israel, troops from Syria, Iraq and Jordan attacked the Zionist State, in order to regain the lands that were seized from the Palestinians. Of all the wars between Arabs and Israelis, the 1948 war, which lasted several months, is considered the longest. At the end Israel emerged victorious and further strengthened its presence in Palestinian soil to extend its expansionist tentacles beyond what had been assigned in the plan of partition of 1948 that of it was completely impartial. The Absolute humiliation feeling that toured every corner of the Middle East could not be hidden. An unknown Arab said that at the end of the war, won't be peace between Arabs and Israelis while the injustice persists on Palestinian people. More than 60 years after, that phrase has maintained according to the vicissitudes of that so gloomy scene.

By Kassem Asmar Castellanos

In this, we have to be careful and not to be carried away by euphemisms that for nothing they had to do with the course of events in the region of the Middle East and in particular Palestine, since that triumph obeyed, basically, to the vertical support of great Britain and the United States with armament much more advanced than those the Arabs had. The aim of this explanation is to question and argue the oversized exaltation that history narrated by Zionists and those who have not taken the effort to make a more serious study about the circumstances that surrounded the defeat of Arabs in the first conflict in 1948. Others went further when said that a hand belonging to the majestic divinity guided by an unique heavenly force, had led the Zionist army to victory. These fictional stories had the goal to show them to international public opinion that the only thing they wanted was to live in peace and who dared to attack them had to face the wrath of the Almighty heavenly.

The Zionists who ventured to make such comparisons; it seems that they were surrounded by certain scourges of amnesia against history, to see that others have not claimed their achievements by alleged aids that came from the eternity. For example; the impressive campaigns of Alexander the great which allowed the release of the Greeks of the Persian scourge and later with successive conquests that reached the Mediterranean shores until the confine of Asia, defeating the Persian Empire which had a powerful army, In addition, to prevent the resurgence of the Persians through the Mediterranean Sea that joined upon territories of the region, Alexander the great conquered Syria, Palestine, and Egypt. So the scope of his conquests from the Greek Mediterranean coasts up to the confines of India, Alexander the great was a conqueror of extraordinary strategic vision and military, but was this an indication of intervention, as support for his conquests, of an immeasurable force from the divine Providence?

By Kassem Asmar Castellanos

I refuse to believe that the Creator of the universe is involved giving support to such fierce military campaigns that the only sure thing, after all, is that leave a murky trail of death, destruction and hatred.

Napoleon Bonaparte before being defeated, capitulated too many armies of the Center and Western Europe, reached even the heart of Moscow, so, was he guided by Divine Providence? Spaniards extended their conquests from the Aztec lands until Argentine soil over more than three centuries .Was that possible, thanks to a Heavenly illumination?

What the reader must know is that for many years, there have been constant strategic cooperation agreements between the United States and Israel where this last one receives huge economic and military assistance. But one of the points where the United States has concurred a solid commitment with the Zionist State in order to secure to Israel that the United States will guarantee, (as it has been doing), the supremacy of Israeli army in the Southwestern Asian region and in particular, on the area of the Middle East with the permanent supply of the most new and deadly weapons of the world such as the famous bombers F17 and other heavy military equipment. Israel receives weapons before NATO, which is the agency responsible of defending the Western world. Specific cases for example; the famous Patriot missiles of technological breakthrough for the interception of missiles from opposite side which were sent to Israel before being seen by the countries belonging to NATO, so Israel is a huge U.S. military base to defend western interests.

By Kassem Asmar Castellanos

AL NAKBA; THE PALESTINIAN CATASTROPHE SPREADS OUT

After the Arabs´ defeat in the war of 1948, the Zionists had the best propitious scenery to extend his cloak of intimidation and conquest over most of the corners of Palestine, anyway, wasn't it referred to in all primers that were taught in different Zionist congresses in Europe?

The harsh reality for the Palestinians is that if it was considered as a misfortune having lost 56% of their territory with the partition plan, after the war of 1948 the geographical map had shown something else for the Zionist State because had control over 78% of the Palestinian territory, in such a way that the adjectives were short to describe the pathetic picture which it reached, especially if you take into account the Palestinian human exodus after the defeat of 1948. So to speak clearly, the real sacrificed were precisely the Palestinians since they lost their lands and if this it was not enough, they couldn't settle in a State and not only that situation but also they were thrown out. In other words, according to the facts, it could not be worse for the Palestinians, the misfortune was total.

After the war, the West Bank (a small territory that was left of Palestine) went to be part of Jordan and many Palestinians expelled by the forces of the Zionist occupation, went there. Gaza Strip, which came to form part of the Egyptian administration, also housed many Palestinians, and another unspecified number of Palestinians had to live in other Arab countries. The figures are eloquent; about 780,000 Palestinians were thrown out of their country, additionally, innumerable Palestinian populations wiped out by Zionist criminal gangs, like in the films of Lawless bandits.

This humanitarian catastrophe was known internationally with the Arabic name of Al- Nakba. This should be understood as the same Arab-Palestinians pointed out the loss of their homes, their lands, and livelihoods. Furthermore to that, they were forced through the Zionist strength and intimidation, to leave all the territories not only which initially had been assigned by the partition plan of 1947 through their British and American henchmen, but also, to the new Palestinian territories that the Zionist expansionism obtained during the war of 1948. Then, Palestine had been reduced to only 22% of its original territory, and the Jews had 78% of the Palestinian area.

So Al-Nakba refers to the exodus undertaken by a large part of the Palestinian people to different directions of the four cardinal points, because there was no other option, go out if you don't want to die! That was a clear Zionist slogan in such a way that to stay in the Palestinian territories meant that it had to be in front of the Zionist bullets therefore many Palestinians preferred to abandon their lands although this decision was very difficult because of the long journey into the unknown was tiring and dangerous. But honoring the truth, for some of the Palestinians, it wasn't easy to take an uncertain course with their children and preferred to stay, what happened to them? What you are going to read is not any content extracted from any horror movie. According the delegate of the International Red Cross Jacques Renoir, with threats and much difficulty visited the village Deir Yassin, after she realized that something had happened there, as soon as she arrived there, was astonished to see the magnitude of the massacre with the use of guns and knives against the inhabitants of Deir Yassin. It is right to clarify that this massacre was given before the partition and the creation of Israel but it is a value for historical reference to show the real ideological intentions of the Zionists, regarding the Palestinian territories.

Data obtained by this delegate of the International Red Cross from first-hand sources and with its presence at the site of the tragic incident said that of the 280 people who were living in the village, barely 50 people survived since they realized the situation before starting the criminal Zionist massacre and were able to flee, otherwise they would have been part of the statistic. But this massacre is not unique because there had been other massacres against the Palestinians even long before. If that happened before the creation of the Zionist State and before the 1948 war, can you imagine what happened to dozens of Palestinian villages once the armed conflict ended that year?

By Kassem Asmar Castellanos

I am convinced that the enclave that wanted to create the "imperialist Western civilization" headed by the British-American partnership in the heart of the Middle East from the beginning contained ,clearly, identifiable purposes of sectarian vision devised in the first Zionist Congress established in Switzerland at the end of the 19th century, since then the unanimous goal wasn't even to find or set up a homeland for the Jews but an absolute expropriation of the whole of Palestine, regardless of the resources and means that should be used. At the end, the speech is always the same in the sense that they are following a "Divine Mandate". Anyway, the permanent Israeli discourse that claims to be the unique democratic State in the Middle East, is nothing more than a racist State that was founded on the Resolution 181 that beforehand had the approbation in a shameless way and with the blatant maneuver of the Americans that with a purely pro-Zionist gesture, handled the central enclosure of the UN as the management given to any brothel. To be honest, today things have not changed much.

To make sure the clearance of Palestinian lands as quick as is possible, bloodthirsty paramilitary groups and Zionist terrorists had been formed for such purpose, whose leaders were Menachem Begin, Yitzhak Shamir, Ben Gurion, Ariel Sharon, and whose hands were covered with blood by the criminal raids that led against many Palestinian villages with the aim of sowing terror and distress to force Arab-Palestinian villagers to flee their homes. Unfortunately, the intentions of those Zionist criminal groups gave result because of, since their first appearances in the Decade of the twenties of the 20th century until the end of 1948; more than one million Palestinians had abandoned their homes and their lands. Naturally, Ben Gurion and his henchmen criminal friends felt more than satisfied towards the size of the performed task. All of them were rewarded with important political positions as sign of gratitude to their "patriotic" jobs in favor of Israel. Even one of them, Menahim Begin, as soon as he signed the peace agreement with Egypt in 1979, was awarded with the Nobel Prize of peace, what a disgrace!

By Kassem Asmar Castellanos

THE ZIONIST DALET PLAN

A group of Zionists led by Ben-Gurion, although within their ranks, there were important personalities like Menachem Begin, Ariel Sharon, Yitzhak Shamir among others, that decades later reached the most important political positions of the Israel's State as the Prime Minister, devised in 1947 a murderous plan of ethnic cleansing, with a large-scale intimidation against the Palestinian populations with the main goal of evicting the largest possible area of Palestine, on the eve of starting the discussion, "seriously" , about the Palestine partition in the UN general Assembly. They saw the need to create terrorist groups of military profile, which could carry out the criminal task of the plan that was brewing. Zionist leaders realized that geographic aspect could influence on this vote and on the other hand they wanted to execute their agenda of creating conditions for the continuous and massive arrival of Jews to Palestine. For such purpose they had to develop a project that will facilitate the expulsion of Palestinians at a faster pace, however was not difficult, taking into account that the Jews had been armed to the teeth, in addition, Zionist organizations from different parts of the world guaranteed to them huge resources. Zionist leaders activated the green light for this new plan in 1947 somewhere in Tel Aviv, that plan was known as Plan Dalet. One of those who participated in its elaboration was Ben Gurion, whose voice did not tremble even an instant when said verbatim: "the main objective of this plan is the systematic destruction of Arab villages and the expulsion of its inhabitants ".

The basis of that plan as a need to fulfill with its aim consisted to compile many information about demographic and geographic topics to have an overview of the Palestinian activities and locations. These criminal groups had the mission of studying each village, recording the number of inhabitants and location of each village, its strategic importance based on its proximity to most important sites for the Zionists, the quality of the land in terms of its fertility, the degree of difficulty in accessing these villages, etc. Once launched the genocidal plan, more than 350 Palestinian villages were literally destroyed and their inhabitants forced to leave Palestine forever. Most populated places by Palestinians that were considered intermediate cities such as Beersaba and others were simply turned into ghost towns,

By Kassem Asmar Castellanos

forcing the Palestinian residents to vacate them. As said Menachem Begin proudly, "we came to the villages as knife on butter". During the second world war, the British trained many of these bloodthirsty murderous who participated in this massive criminal act.

The plan was to bulldoze those villages closest to the Jewish concentrations, for thus gradually move forward, according to the degree of priority. This task of human eviction could be accomplished, easily, through the absence of observers and media correspondents, simply because the Zionist leaders forbade them to prevent international public opinion didn't get any information about the Zionist atrocities against the Palestinian population. Those who dared to document the facts for further dissemination to the rest of the world simply could have a much risk of being murdered. This tragic fate happened to a famous figure known as Count Folke Bernadotte who was chosen by the UN in May 1948 to draft a report according to his own observation in the heart of Palestine. Obviously, taking into account the atrocities and Zionist violations against the Palestinians and clear indications about the expulsion of many Palestinians from their homes. In order to avoid this report in the UN, Count Folke was vilely assassinated in the occupied territories. Today the Zionist behavior does not differ from which they wielded for more than 70 years ago to avoid that the world knows, accurately what happens within the borders of the occupied territories, because always the Zionists attempt to hide their crimes.

By Kassem Asmar Castellanos

THE ZIONIST ATTEMPT TO HIDE THEIR CRIMES

Israel, before facts and statistics so forceful and heartbreaking as a result of the criminal acts in a sequential manner against Palestinian populations, before, during and after the period of 1948, has tried by all means to restrict the information through the misinformation and distortion of facts in order to gain the solidarity of the international community and thus move from victimizer to victim, arguing that all they were doing was to defend themselves from the constant Arab attacks. This kind of speeches, usually, is used by Zionists, not only in Israel but in everywhere, and this it has not even been alien to the 21st century. One of the speeches that is prefabricated and false which Israel likes showing it, is about the facts of the Al-Nakba and the Dalet Plan, when they say Palestinian exodus that occurred at that time had its cause and origin to the recommendations of the Arab leaders to the Arab-Palestinians in that area in order to prevent a collateral effect that could affect them because according to that deformed report, it was brewing an attack against Jews in large scale. A few years later, studies of various European committees noted that they didn't find any evidence that could corroborate the Zionist assertion. So this is one of many tactics that the Zionist State of Israel has tried to use in order to reverse the course of historical events, with the manipulation of records and data that are fully identified that explain the development of the facts as they occurred in the Palestinian territories. But the insolence of the Zionist disinformation goes further, saying that the villages and Palestinian Arab population of that era existed, but in extremely subtle quantities. This manipulation tactic through the media, was uncovered when Israeli revisionists and Palestinian historians started the task of making a serious investigative study, based on sources of first-rate documentation in order to show to the world public what had always ensured not only the Palestinians, but also the independent historians.

Salman Abu Sitta known analyst and researcher, had determined to make an investigation about the torment that the Palestinian people lived, especially in relation to the looting and expulsion that suffered. Own data and from other researchers, such as the Palestinian Professor Walid Al Jalidid, and indirectly by the Israeli historian Benny Morris whose sincerity in his writing

By Kassem Asmar Castellanos

encompasses a mind with enormous cynicism and human insensitivity that project an unhealthy style of presentation and justification around the most barbaric and criminal conduct. The only "favor" that Benny Morris has made for the Palestinian cause is to have recognized that the Nakba, as the Palestinians described it, and the criminal acts against many Palestinian villages were carried out by the direct orders of Ben Gurion.

Through his book "The Origin of the Problem of Palestinian Refugees", Morris assumes a disconcerting attitude by saying that the argument of the Zionists in the sense that the Palestinians left their lands voluntarily in 1948 following the advice of some Arab leaders, is not true and corroborates that the hundreds of thousands of Palestinians who formed this exodus into exile, was because of the hostilities from Zionist militias. This controversial Israeli historian said that there was an ethnic cleansing on a large scale through massacres, rape, evictions and tactics of sophisticated intimidation to scare the Palestinians in order to expel them from their homes. But the most surprising thing about his book is the way how he justifies all these atrocious acts against the Palestinians, indicating it as very necessary for the Foundation of the State of Israel. In fact, he ensures that the orders came directly from Ben Gurion and supported what he did.

This Israeli historian whose conduct seems like an inveterate sociopath, said that Ben Gurion was wrong to not expel all Palestinians from their lands, in fact, continues supporting the idea of a new Palestinian exodus by force. Benny Morris said that to achieve the goal of creating a homeland for the Jews in Palestine, it was necessary to use all the resources, i.e. "the end justifies the means". One of his most famous interventions was given in an interview with a major informational medium in Israel where he said: "a Jewish State would not have existed without the uprooting of 700,000 Palestinians; therefore it was necessary to uproot them, as also the ethnic cleansing was necessary". Continues this misfit man, suggesting a strong nuclear attack on Iran in such a way that is reduced in a bleak and desolate desert if not stop his nuclear program. And to think that this historian permanently gives talks at Hebrew universities of Israel over the conflict in the Middle East.

By Kassem Asmar Castellanos

Returning to job that assumed the renowned researcher Salman Abu Sitta, who taking advantage also of the opening of the Israeli secret files related with the founding of the State of Israel and from there, he could extract what was known but this time the great importance is that this information didn't come from Arab records but from the Zionist source that incessantly, through several decades had denied the content of this kind of events in the Palestinian territories.

The job that Abu Sitta had done was included in a book with the title "Al-Nakba 1948: registry of people evicted in Palestine". That document evidences the vast plan of assault over the Palestinian territories as the central axis of the ambitions of the Zionist organizations to create a unique and exclusive home for Jews, showing the spirit of the future Zionist nation that should be strictly governed by a racist dogma. In These files he could find irrefutable evidences that the territory was indeed populated by Arab- Palestinians and not as the Jews sought to show that they were uninhabited lands. Another very important fact was that at the beginning of the 20th century, Muslims, Jews and Christians coexisted without any mishap in Palestine until began to arise problems with the arrival of the first Jewish immigrants in order to start to comply with the dark and evil plans of the Zionist organizations to take over Palestine, in fact through that work, he could find out that as soon as the Palestinians were being evicted, were systematically replaced by Jewish immigrants and thus try to redesign in hidden and unnoticed way the demographic and geographic context of Palestine. The famous Zionist military Moshe Dayan recognized that the majority of Jews' places were built over Arab towns.

These Zionist plans were drawn with the aim that its applicability was quick and sequential, having into account many important facts such as:

a) To take advantage of the feeling of solidarity from the most powerful countries by the suffering caused by the Nazi Holocaust.

b) To take advantage of the presence of the British power in Palestine, such as administrator and involve them to the Zionist plan, as indeed happened with the Balfour Declaration.

c) To broadcast a constant lie to the world that Palestine belongs to them by "Divine Mandate" and that is a historical fact inherent to the Jewish race and its right to return to Palestine.

d) The Zionist organizations had assumed the task of providing a radical pedagogy among the Jews who lived in different countries to convince them that all means were valid to evict the Arab-Palestinian inhabitants of Palestine.

The result of this research was not a surprise for the Palestinians, because they had this statistical data and information sources since many years ago, on the events that surrounded the prior months to the creation of the State of Israel as after the beginning of the first Arab-Israeli war in 1948.

In summary, according this investigative job, the number of villages, towns and small Arab towns and taking into account that some parts were evicted, but others simply destroyed, totaled approximately 380.

At the end of 1947 and the start of 1948, in a record period of five months, this Zionist groups had gotten to scare away more Palestinians than the entire previous period since the beginning of the Jewish migration. In fact the objective of the Plan Dalet was precisely that goal and its main ringleader who was Ben Gurion had explained it in more than one occasion to encourage all their supporters to take over the maximum extension possible of the Palestinian territory, being understood this message as the totality of the "promised land", demonstrating blatant form the racist ideology not only of Ben Gurion but of all those who were part of the plans established by the Zionist leaders. They felt very confident and safe in applying convincingly the Zionist thought when they found a new support on the international stage after the second World War, following the unconditional support they had received from British, support that consisted of exaggerated assistance in weapons, financial assistance and political back up that came from the United States of America.

The huge farce that Zionist Jews sought to show is that they had accepted the partition plan on the eve of 1948, which Arabs had rejected. Well, that is true, but the story should not be shown in pieces and much less biased. The fact is that Arabs rejected the

By *Kassem Asmar Castellanos*

plan just like any other society or people could have rejected it, regardless whether they are Arab or not, we have to remember that it was assigned to a Jewish minority that didn't pass the third part of the inhabitants of Palestine in demographic terms, 56% of the Palestinian territory. That's not all, the Jews just had 10% of the territory then it was evident in the eyes of anyone that the partition plan had been designed with a misleading approach to promote the strategies drawn up by Zionism. Was not enough to reject it? It would be ridiculous that the Jews wouldn't accept the partition plan! But what comes next is blatantly amazing verging any degree of humiliation against the Palestinian people when openly manifested Ben Gurion that "to build a Jewish State immediately, even if it is not throughout the territory, the rest will come with time. It has to come." Then the question was not if the Arabs were to agree or not with the partition of Palestine, but that the Zionist leadership had already designed, meticulously, a roadmap in order to take over of the whole Palestinian territories. Remember that Ben Gurion, a first line fanatic, was a Zionist activist without having fulfilled the age of majority because at the age of 17 he was honored to be a member of Zionism. It was quite clear to say that the only way to occupy the entire Palestinian territory is through the force, so he devised ambitious plans before the end of the Second World War to arm the Jewish people with sophisticated weapons because it had the firm conviction, in fact it was so, that through that road it could ensure the expansionism. During this period, he made strategic agreements with Great Britain and France in the economic and military fields, later Israel signed special agreements of strategic cooperation with the United States for the purpose of arming excessively the Zionist State and ensure its expansionism. This cooperation continues nowadays.

MOODS ARE EXACERBATED

The scene that was possible to see at the end of 1948, from an optical angle of Zionism indicated that everything was going on smoothly, but as a result of the escalation of injustices that had been committed against the Palestinian people since the beginning of the 20th century until the epilogue of 1948, where it carried out the mass expulsion of Palestinians from their homes, historic and painful fact known as Al-Nakba, which meant a continuous chain of abuses and Zionist aggressions against the Palestinian people, eventually triggered a feeling of anger and impotence. These events led to a disturbing fact that inevitably started to flow with force on the stage of the region and particularly in the emotional spirit of the Arabs, which, by the way, a total humiliation. That disturbing fact that is maintained until today, gave rise to a feeling of hatred and resentment at that time, because of the extent of the changes that the events were taking in that part of the Middle East that ended up affecting to Palestinians.

After the defeat of the Arabs in the 1948 war, psychosis gripped the Jews who lived in different Arab countries for fear of reprisals against their communities. Without trying to prove what happened under any circumstances with Jews who resided in various Arab countries and honoring the truth, part of them began to receive abuse and discrimination, not by Arab societies but the authorities themselves. The majority of these Jews lived in the southwest of the region in countries such as Yemen and Iraq, and to a lesser extent in Syria. Jews belonging to North Africa came from Morocco, Egypt and Libya.

Israel took advantage of this situation and did everything that was at its disposal to bring the Arab Jews to the newly created Israel. It was not difficult because the Arab Jewish community at this time was with constant fear of possible retaliation by Arab Governments of the countries in question, and so it was easy for them to have taken the decision of living permanently in Israel. In the period between 1948 and 1952, more than a half million Arab Jews had reached the "promised land ". The migration of Jews to Palestine never stopped because the invitations from the authorities of Israel and the World Zionist movement were always present in their agenda. This fact not only puts in doubt the false assertion of Zionism that the problem of Arabs and Palestinians in particular is a religious issue, but also discards that theory by demonstrating that for many years lived, side by side, Muslims, Jews and Christians without major inconveniences. The problem began to emerge as a result of the constant territorial plunder that the Arab-Palestinians began to see in the early 20th century obeying a plan orchestrated by the Zionists.

The Zionist movements at the beginning of the 20th century, always understood the importance of the demographic data as a political weapon on the world stage, to such point of shamelessness that as soon as the world entered the 20th century, these Jewish nationalist organizations started to distort statistics in the demographic field over Palestinian territories because of the media technology and the displacement of the data was quite slow, although most countries did not believe in the statistical information that the Zionists were showing about the population composition of the Palestinian territories at the beginning of the 20th. The argument that wielded the Zionist organizations at that time, it referred that Palestine was almost completely uninhabited when the first Jewish migrations from Europe arrived. Evidently, today no one believes in such deception and lying to such a point that the Israelis themselves do not dare to talk about it. The Zionists and later Israel, with the alteration of the demographic data, tried to "legitimize" continuous robberies and looting of Palestinian lands.

Between 1905 and 1920, data and statistical provisions showed that Arab-Palestinians formed 90% of the Palestinian territories, while the Jews were only 10% of the population. The following figures which show the evolution of the population's composition over Palestinian territories throughout the 20th century, are more than eloquent and show the intention of the "Zionist spirit" to populate as quickly as possible those lands of the Middle East which had been inhabited by Palestinians for centuries. In early 1914, records of credible sources indicated that there were 55,000 Jews and more than 630,000 Palestinians, i.e. 92% of the population in Palestine were Palestinians and only 8% were Jews. Almost a century later, of the total population living in Israel, the West Bank and the Gaza Strip (don't forget that all these lands

By Kassem Asmar Castellanos

belonged to the Palestinians until 1947) that are approximately 9.7 million inhabitants, two-thirds are Israeli citizens, although it is relevant to clarify that 530,000 Jewish settlers live in illegal settlements scattered through the West Bank.

Certainly those so abrupt changes in the demographic field that was developed between early 20th century and early 21st century, was not given by the grace of a simple mysterious coincidence, but they reflected the same dynamics of the social processes, demographic and geographic that the Zionists and the State of Israel imposed with violence, using any method or mechanism to achieve that goal, with the conspiracy and shameful support of both British and Americans.

In 1920, there were 70,000 Jews and 670,000 Palestinians. At the next decade of the 1930s, it is considered as an important stage for the Zionist aspirations of populating Palestine with Jews citizens coming from many parts of Europe. This decade was special because contributed with approximately 230,000 Jews, most of them were living in the countries of Eastern Europe such as Russia, Poland and Romania, and this trend continued basically until the end of the thirties of the 20th century, when other Jews from Germany and England joined to this "special invitation" to occupy foreign territory. In 1930, there was a statistical record that showed that the population in Palestine was 740,000 Palestinians and 150,000 Jews, these numbers indicate that in just 16 years, i.e. from 1914 until 1930 Jews passed representing 8% of the population to be 17% of population on Palestinian soil.

Obviously the thirst of the Zionist organizations to populate Palestinian territories with Jews, it could not satisfy but with constant migrations and the evolution of the figures as passed the years so it looked because in 1940 the Jews had on Palestinian soil 430,000 inhabitants and the Palestinians during this period totaled 1,100,000 inhabitants, this new data sped up the alarms in the Palestinian territories because of in a period of 25 years, the Jewish population went from 8% to 29% of the total population of Palestine. From 1940, followed increasing Jewish migration, obeying two phenomenon:

By Kassem Asmar Castellanos

a) The same Zionist strategy to promote increasingly, Jewish migration from everywhere of Europe.

b) Taking advantage of the persecution of the Nazi regime to continue justifying their presence in Palestine, sending more Jewish citizens.

There is a historical record of the beginning of World War II, which uncovered the deception of the Zionists, in order to seize Palestine. Although no one denies that they were subjected through persecution and murders by the violent regime of Hitler, but it is essential to clarify that the Zionists took advantage of this historical moment to encourage migration to Palestine. There were dozens of countries that were willing to accommodate Jews, why they insisted to migrate to Palestinian territories? Well, the answer is not so difficult because of this entire event obeyed to the Zionist strategy of a homeland for the Jews in Palestine and at the end; they took advantage of this historical situation.

In late 1947 and early 1948, i.e. on the eve of the founding of the Zionist State, there were registers of nearly 300 Jewish settlements in Palestine with many Jewish settlers. Obviously the English were responsible for this series of migration and in particular, with the famous Balfour Declaration.

In 1948, Palestinians were approximately 1,430,000 inhabitants but several correlated factors redesigned the demographic aspect of the place, markedly. Those factors were the Dalet Plan, the Foundation of the State of Israel, the 1948 Arab-Israeli war and the Palestinian exodus known as Al - Nakba. It is important to remember that between 1947 and mid-1948, more than 820,000 Palestinians had been forced to leave their homes.

In the 21th century, the migration to Israel and the occupied territories is on the daily agenda of the Israeli government and the only need to set up permanent residence in Palestine is professing the Jewish religion.

By Kassem Asmar Castellanos

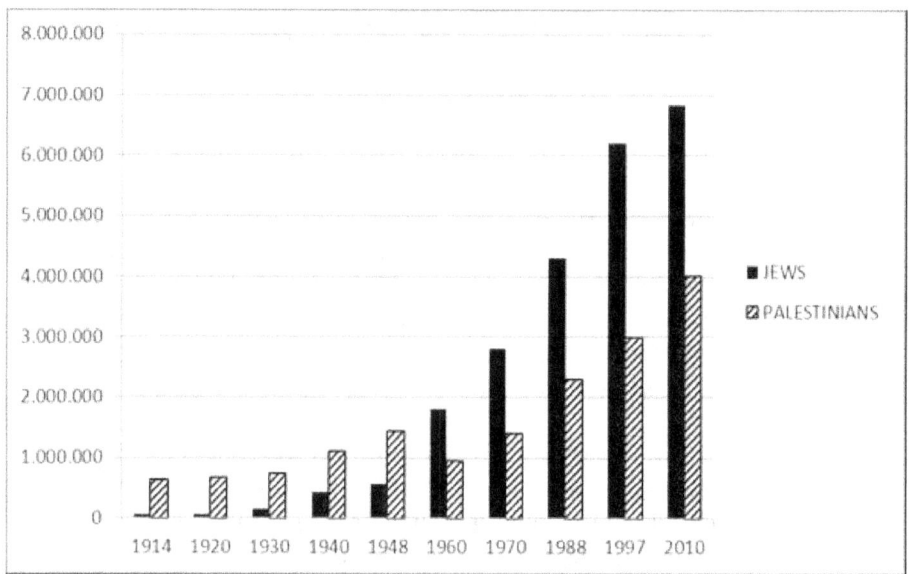

Graphic 1. Demographic evolution in the region

By Kassem Asmar Castellanos

2. THE ISRAELI EXPANSIONISM, AS AN EXCUSE TO CONTROL THE WATER RESOURCES AND THE THEFT OF LANDS

Although, there are strong indications that the Zionist organizations at the beginning of the 20th century with the first Jewish migrations to Palestine, had already focused on the importance of ensuring water sources in the region to stimulate agricultural activities for the first contingents of Jews in Palestine, those intentions were much more marked after the establishment of Israel in 1948.

The main aim that led Israel to occupy the Golan Heights was the question of water over the issue of security. In fact, Moshe Dayan said that Israel in 1967 provoked Syria to get involved in the war in order to have the pretext to occupy that territory, because more than a quarter of the water that Israel consumes comes from the Syrian territory of the Golan Heights, reason by which, the Israelis today do not show interest to engage in peace talks with the Government of Syria because is Israel the beneficiary of this whole story.

I am convinced that 1967 war was devised by Israel in response to its expansionist ideology and incidentally to ensure new territories with their valuable water sources, because the statements not only by Moshe Dayan, but also of other important personalities of the political and military sphere of Israel, corroborate it. For example who was the Commander of the Israeli air force, General Ezer Weizmann acknowledged that Egypt, Syria and Jordan showed no serious threat against Israel, but they had to weaken them in anyway.

Menachem Begin agreed with the above statements by saying that Israel decided to start the war, attacking the Arab armies. Yitzhak Shamir didn't stay behind with their statements given few months after the war of 1967, when he said that Egypt did not show serious intentions of attacking Israel because it was sure of its military superiority in terms of weapons quality and especially his supremacy that represented its air force, backed by aircraft fighters acquired from Britain, France and the United States as were the famous Miraj and Phantom, therefore the Zionist army

By Kassem Asmar Castellanos

had no rival from the air force of Syria or Egypt and the intention was to not allow that in the future those armies could be effective, moreover for Israel to keep up the supremacy of the Israeli Army became a permanent priority, mainly being supported by its strategic partner the United States.

After this war, Israel began to occupy the Golan Heights and as usual with its expansionist policy, reached to expel 100,000 Syrians from their homes with different methods of intimidation. Under that practice, The Syrians who could stay in that region were few.

Today, about 40,000 inhabitants live in the Golan Heights, of which half are Jewish colonists with Israeli passports that have special privileges in the illegal settlements where they live, in that sense the Syrians who live on the plateau of the Golan, which are about 20,000, have to buy the water to an unreasonably higher cost in comparison with the cost paid by the Jewish colonists. Needless to clarify that this measure, also applies to the West Bank and Gaza that obeys to a strategy that holds a cynical purpose of pressure against the legitimate owners of those territories. It is a clear sign that Israel continues with its policy of discrimination, as in the occupied territories of West Bank and Gaza. Syrian natives of the Golan Heights do not escape these racist measures.

The present data indicates that the Israeli consumption of water per person daily is about 260 liters while the use of the Palestinians of the occupied territories hardly reaches 60 liters. But the Palestinians that are furthest, such as those who live in villages and agricultural areas, often cannot enjoy 20 liters of water per person.   The difference widens if we take into account that more than 300,000 Jewish colonists (not counting East Jerusalem settlers) who live in more than 150 illegal settlements in the occupied territories, since they are pampered with a lot more water than the Palestinians, owners of the land where the settlements are, and this in order that they stay in the colonies.

Nowadays, the data handled by international agencies confirm that Israel takes advantage of 80% of the water that passes through the West Bank. Many Palestinians must withstand tortuous rationing of water that extends throughout the summer,

By Kassem Asmar Castellanos

but do not suffer that measure the inhabitants of Israel, and much less the Jewish inhabitants who live in the illegal settlements throughout the occupied territories. Because of the need of this vital liquid, many Palestinians have to resort to tanker trucks to buy some water. The situation becomes more difficult for those Palestinians who live away from the urban centers, as in fields where the most are farmers who need that precious liquid for two main reasons; that are for family consumption and obviously for agricultural activities.

The Palestinians who live in the refugee camps, suffer too much from the rationing imposed by Israel. It should be emphasized that the little water that arrive in Gaza is awful. If we add the strong impediment imposed by Israel for water from the West Bank does not get there, in addition to this, the Palestinians cannot build wells to collect water without the express permission of the authorities of Israel. Israel wants to keep up a climate of hopelessness and frustration. For example in Gaza, it is extremely difficult the entry of equipment for water treatment because Israel alleges "security issues". The Palestinians have to undergo, within its territory, to the measures imposed by the Israeli occupation forces, creating feelings of helplessness.

Palestinians cannot use the roads next to the illegal Jewish settlements in the occupied territories but according to Israel due to "security issues", and only Jewish colonists can do it. This measure since 1967 has damaged much the Palestinians because they have to make a longer journey to bring not only water but also goods to different places in the occupied territories or vice versa. It seems that thanks to this pair of words "security issues", Israel has taken too much advantage for the benefit of its citizens and this has happened in the last 45 years. In fact, these State policies that Israel arbitrarily has been imposing to a great part of Palestinians who live in the occupied territories of the West Bank, has forced many Palestinian families being coerced to handle a domestic economy which does not extend beyond the threshold of subsistence, because they cannot cultivate but a small part of land and the same thing happens when the Palestinians want to raise a few sheep due to with the limited amount of water, this kind of farming activities cannot be expanded.

By Kassem Asmar Castellanos

Without a doubt it's the traditional tactics of Israel to make fall these Palestinian communities in a state of frustration and helplessness in order that they leave these lands, with the aim to build more illegal Jewish settlements to accommodate new Jewish colonists from many countries.

If we consider a significant part of Palestinian communities in the occupied territories is dedicated to the activities of the field as farming and breeding of goats and sheep, it is extremely difficult to keep these tasks under continuous water rationing. While that happens with many Palestinians, most Jewish colonists who live in illegal settlements have swimming pools. International Amnesty has been emphatic in demanding to Israel to put endpoint to its discriminatory policy in terms of distribution of water where evidence clearly, the privileges of the Jewish colonists in comparison with the Palestinian population of the occupied territories. Moreover, this international organism asks the Israeli Government to suspend the blockade that weighs on the Gaza Strip because it hinders the arrival of equipment to repair and build water infrastructures. On the other hand, the UN has said that Israel consumes most of its water, resources that do not belong to the 1948 borders but to the territories of 1967, especially those from the West Bank. It must also take into account that Israel extracts water from the plateau of the Golan Heights, territory that belongs to Syria, but that is under Israeli occupation since 1967.

The South of Lebanon was under Israeli occupation for more than 20 years (1978-2000) to stop attacks from several Palestinian and Lebanese factions towards Israeli populations. But once more, the issue of "security of Israel" was well exploited by the Hebrew State, since they did not stop during this time range to carry water to Israel from the Litany River that is the most famous Lebanese river. This was the main argument that had Israel to occupy the South of Lebanon for so many years. Always, Israel wants to take advantage with the question of security that became a particular Israeli excuse. Israel always seeks pretexts to steal resources from those who have border with the Jewish State. In order to continue benefiting of the Litany River´s waters in Lebanon, the Zionists showed the pretext of the abduction of two Israeli soldiers in 2006 by Hezbollah and undertook a savage military operation

By Kassem Asmar Castellanos

on a massive scale, causing much destruction and death in Lebanon (1200 civilians dead) but the main objective was to take advantage of the crystalline waters of Litany River. Is it not a racist and criminal act, which is carried out a unilateral military escalation against a country, causing desolation in its territory by two soldiers abducted?

If we take into account all of this, the figures show us that of all the water that Israel consumes, 65% doesn't belong to its territory. With these numbers, those who benefit most of this vital liquid are Israeli citizens and Jewish colonists of the illegal settlements in the West Bank. This explains the constant mockery that Israel has exhibited against the peace process and the international community. Another proof that confirms this is the constant Israeli rejection when doesn't allow to the Palestinian Authority to take part in the management of this valuable water resource. Another aspect that makes it difficult for Palestinians to get access to water is the excessive price of it, because there is a discriminatory measure by the authorities of Israel. Palestinian residents of the West Bank pay the price of water, with exaggerated rates, while Israeli colonists who live in illegal settlements in the occupied territories, get water with a lower cost.

So, the Israeli occupation is not only reflected in physical military presence in the occupied territories, but also because they have become looters of the Palestinian natural resources. In the peace talks between both sides, Israel has postponed any dialog about the issue of water knowing that in the current circumstances, with the occupying force, he is taking full advantage and will continue to do so while the international community continues assuming that poor and static role of simple Viewer, accompanied by occasional verbal condemnations.

As it had mentioned in this book, in any peace negotiations between Israeli and Palestinian representatives, the Palestinians have to go very concentrated with the issue of water resources, especially if we have into account that many of the Palestinians earn their everyday life in agriculture and at the same time supply to an important part of the Palestinian people in the West Bank and Gaza.

By *Kassem Asmar Castellanos*

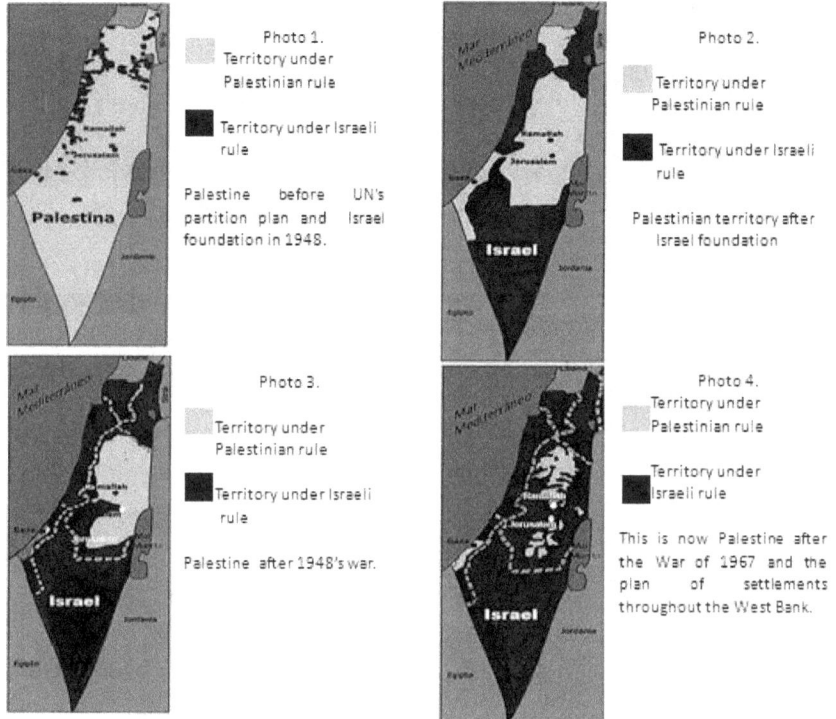

Photo 1. Source: The clinic on line-16 november,2012   (adapted)

But historical data show that interest in the water comes from strategies planned since the beginning of the 20th century, where the Zionists, unscrupulous, wanted to take control of the Litany River of Lebanon but this time, France which was the occupying power of Syria and Lebanon opposed outright, anyway, the stratagem of the Zionist Jews were always focused beyond the borders of 1948 to add more water sources. This ambition of great insolence and cynicism, has remained even into the 21th century, because the Israeli State always encourages the Jews that are living in everywhere of the world to go to live in the occupied territories therefore, Israel wish to ensure enough water. This means that water issue always will be a thorny issue because the Israeli authorities want to ensure the vital liquid to supply their Jewish colonists living in the illegal West Bank settlements and to their citizens who are in Israeli territory, so even if they have to go

By Kassem Asmar Castellanos

on the rights of the Palestinians who have been living for centuries in West Bank and Gaza. Remember that many of these Jewish colonists and those who live in Israel do not have but a few years in Palestine. Most of them were born, grew up and lived many years in other countries mainly in Europe, however in light of the Israeli viewpoint, they have more right than the Palestinians by the mere fact that they profess the Jewish religion.

We must point out that the only fact that many Israeli citizens and Jews settlers who live in Israel and in illegal settlements in the occupied territories, obliges the Zionist authorities of Israel to give them with most of the prerogatives for fear that if at one point given, those citizens and Jewish colonists do not feel comfortable in Israel, particularly in the occupied territories they can take the determination to return to their countries where they were born and grew up and that is what Israel wants to avoid.

In short, the policy of discrimination imposed by the military authorities of Israel consists of first: to satisfy the requirements of Israeli citizens and their Jewish colonists with the provision of essential services, especially water and electricity in enough quantities with cost that means clear privilege. Apparently the Zionist authorities see with much less concern the Palestinian demand for those services. That was a Zionist strategy for decades consisted of limiting the basic services significantly to Palestinians to pressure them to leave their homes.

It must be clarified that the territories where it founded Israel in 1948, more those territories which were occupied in the wars of 1948 and 1967 respectively, unfortunately meant a very difficult situation for the Palestinians because the panorama had shown that the Zionist State finally ended occupying 100% of Palestine and naturally the task was accomplished according to the dreams of the most prominent Zionist leaders like Ben Gurion and Theodor Herzel. Therefore since 1967 in those Territories militarily occupied by Israel, it had devised Apartheid policies in order to support the Jewish colonists who began to populate the first illegal settlements, which Israel took the determination to build in the occupied territories. Not only it was violating, flagrantly the Palestinian sovereignty but also they began to plunder the Palestinian water resources, diverting its waters in order to supply it to the new colonists and their subjects of Israel.

By Kassem Asmar Castellanos

In that sense, if we take into account that since both parties sat at the first peace conference for the Middle East, held in Madrid in 1991 and up to the date of today, it has already passed more than 20 years and the issue of water and its handling by the authorities of the State of Israel, it has not yet had notable change. Indeed is simply vital and urgent the dismantling of all Zionist settlements that are scattered in the occupied territories of West Bank, otherwise, for a future Palestinian State, it would be very harmful to the quality of Palestinians´ life. It must be understood that those 520,000 Jewish colonists (including East Jerusalem) spend more water than all Palestinian residents in the occupied territories and that is totally unacceptable not only for Palestinians but also by the international community and by the same International Amnesty. So the problem for Palestinians is rather delicate because it transcends the political aspect to socio-economical.

Another fact that must also be taken into account is that in the future, the Palestinians can no longer be subordinated to the intransigent policy of Israel, essentially in the use of services as the electricity and water. The humiliation that accompanies the Palestinians daily is that it has become an issue in fact implausible, when they can't build a simple well for the storage of water in the occupied territories since it must first pass a request to the military authorities of Israel and wait for the response. Many of these requests are rejected and the few that are successful, it must comply several requirements and conditions for example the size of the well and especially the depth of it. On that last point is pretty clear, the discrimination against Palestinians because of the permissions granted to those Palestinians who were "benefited" in order to build a well, the depth of these wells are lower than the ones which the Jewish colonists can build.

About that point, recently the French Deputy Jean Glavanny led a delegation to carry out a serious study of first-hand to be presented to the Committee on Foreign Affairs of the National Assembly of France. This delegation found so much discrimination from the authorities of Israel in the management of the issue of water that the head of the French delegation did not hesitate to use the word Apartheid for the preparation of his report.

By Kassem Asmar Castellanos

After the delegation landed in Israel, they visited many places including the occupied territories of West Bank and Gaza (although in theory Israel withdrew from Gaza, their daily life is still influenced directly by the siege, blockade and discriminatory measures as strong rationing of electricity and water against its inhabitants, also, the high price of these services). The members of that delegation were put to the task of investigating, interviewing different Israeli and Palestinian personalities of different diplomatic sectors, also they listened the opinions of representatives from different NGOs and came to the conclusion that the term Apartheid although causes much commotion within Israel, perfectly it fit to what they had seen and found. Those inquiries that were reflected in the report of the French delegation said that the use of the word Apartheid in the report is related with the discriminatory practices, because Israel applies racist rules that end up pleasing the Jewish citizens and Jewish settlers of the settlements that are in the occupied territories, to detriment of the Palestinian well-being. The word Apartheid irritates too much to Israel and previously, the Zionist State had experimented this kind of feeling with the content of the book written by the former President of the United States Jimmy Carter when he published his literary work "Palestine: peace and not Apartheid" which reached to enrage the authorities of Israel and the Zionist movements in Europe and the United States.

Although the French report does not provide new data different to the ones the Palestinian officials had, unfortunately through Israeli propaganda and international Zionism, the Palestinian reports were considered oversized. Therefore the merit of the French report is that being a friendly country of Israel, dared to reveal through this report, the practices of Apartheid by the Israeli State against the Palestinians and this result is seen with a particular credibility by the international community. Proof of this, the information which is recorded in this report, shows that the Jewish settlers who live in illegal settlements in the West Bank, spend more water than the 2.4 million Palestinians in the West Bank and Gaza. If this is not a clear indication of Apartheid, what another term should be registered with?

By Kassem Asmar Castellanos

Another important information of this Delegation, had confirmed the allegations that the Palestinians were doing, relating to wells that humble people had built without the permission of the Israeli authorities for agricultural work, which ended up being destroyed without contemplation, by the military authorities of the occupying forces.

It is very eloquent the description done by Stephanie Oudot who is the head of projects in the region that belongs to a French organization on the question of water development, referring how the Jewish colonists waste water in swimming pools and gardens while near them, the Palestinians should extract the water from wells. In conclusion, Israel is ,always, taking advantage with the argument "security of Israel", focusing as a main objective the control of water resources beyond its borders known on the demarcation of the green line that the UN had set in 1949.

The little interest of Israel in the peace talks, (although tries to say the opposite), is reflected in the slow progress between Israelis and Palestinians during the past 20 years of conversations. Israel knows that its situation in respect of international legality is very committed and the only tactic that has, is to blame the leaders of Hamas for the failures of those dialogs.

By Kassem Asmar Castellanos

3. JEWISH SETTLEMENTS IN THE OCCUPIED TERRITORIES, THE MOST DIFFICULT OBSTACLE TO REACH A PEACE AGREEMENT

In order that the readers have a clearer image about the meaning of settlements, it is suitable to illustrate the explanation of them. Settlements are small communities, neighborhoods and enclosed spaces full of housing with its own social and economic activities that Israel took the determination to build illegally in the occupied territories of the West Bank, East Jerusalem and the Golan Heights. These settlements from the start had the objective of encouraging Jewish migrations from different parts of the world, mainly from Europe to ensure the Israeli occupation. Although these migrations to Palestine had begun with the plan of the World Zionist movement and the British support at the beginning of the 20th century, this illegal activity took particular intensity after the Israeli occupation of the Palestinian and Syrian territories in 1967.

Their sizes vary, there are settlements from 1,000 to 30,000 inhabitants. The recognized Jewish author Ellen Cantarow that has made several works about the dark Israeli purpose of filling the Palestinian occupied territories, with Jewish settlements. She was a witness of the exaggerated rate of colonization of the West Bank and East Jerusalem through a systematic and methodical policy of expropriation and destruction of Palestinian homes and looting on a massive scale of the Palestinian water sources. The investigative work of Cantarow deserves a particular credibility, since she has made direct interviews with everyone involved with Jewish settlements (both victims as victimizers). Even she could interview many Jew settlers and prominent figures from different trends of Israeli leadership, many of them are right-wing radical politicians. She also had the opportunity to meet many Palestinian villagers to know first-hand the abuses that have lived by the horrible colonization policies carried out by the occupying forces.

By Kassem Asmar Castellanos

Ellen Cantarow was amazed when came to the conclusion after seeing how Israel builds very quickly, settlements across the Palestinian territories. Has denounced the declarations that Israeli leaders have given where they affirm that the purpose of the harsh rules and treatments that apply against the Palestinians have the mission of despairing them to force the Palestinian people to abandon their lands.

She informed the International community about a murky and Machiavellian Plan, which came to public light in 1979, whose primary personage was the head of a Zionist organization whose specialization was to colonize the occupied territories with Jewish settlements, his name Matityahu Drobles. What did this perverse figure propose? Using as pretext the particular interpretations of the Scriptures and take it as an excuse to build settlements around most cities such as Hebron, Bethlehem, Nablus, the East part of Jerusalem and all the ancient and historic Palestinian places, filling them with Jews settlers not only in its periphery, but also in the own gates of these cities, in other words, inside the Palestinian towns. In this way, according to his own racist vision and expansionist spirit, in the future (remember that this plan was developing in 1979, known as Plan Drobles) the Palestinians will become a palpable minority and additionally subordinated to the Israeli political maneuvers, regardless if there are or not peace plans.

Today, this dark Zionist figure should feel quite satisfied because with his collaboration, there are more than 150 illegal settlements in the occupied territories which are home for more than 520,000 Jewish colonists from many parts of the world, moreover, the stolen agricultural lands and the control of water from the surface and subsurface of the Palestinian territories, to keep up a privileged life for these Jewish settlers.

"Drobles Plan" that honors the name of its inventor and author comes from a mentality that was to the service of the apartheid policy of the Israeli State. Remember that Matityahu Drobles was an active member of the Knesset (Israeli Parliament) in the 1970s and his main job was to be creative and strategist in the colonization of the occupied territories through the construction of illegal Jewish settlements on a large scale in these areas. While he was a member of the Knesset until 1977, he always belonged to Zionist movements whose mission and vision was always the expansionism in the occupied territories.

Another important Zionist figure no less harmful, known with the name of Yigal Alon who was active member in the Israeli parliament (Knesset) for more than 20 years. At the end of the 60s this Zionist put to consideration of his government a proposal known as "Alon Plan". In short, what he suggested with his plan is that Israel could reach a peace agreement with the Palestinians but the Zionist state should take over the third part of the west Bank, including East Jerusalem and populate them with Jewish settlements. So it is not strange these facts than bind all these Zionist figures because they share the same expansionist and racist vision.

The first rule that Israel violated when occupied the West Bank, Gaza Strip and the Golan Heights was the Rome Statute of the International Criminal Court and the IV Geneva Convention, which its contents are very explicit in the sense that no occupation force can populate the occupied territory and much less incite displacements for this purpose, because naturally goes against International humanitarian law.

The problem is that practically, it's difficult to condemn Israel while it continues being protected by its eternal partner which is the United States because the only thing that gets is to foster impunity and injustice against the Palestinians. There are many international laws and rules that corroborate the illegality that the Jews settlements represent in Palestinian and Syrian lands. Resolutions 446, 478 and 497, which were adopted by the UN Security Council, are clear in its content. The Resolution 446 considers illegal the construction and presence of settlements in the territories that Israel occupied in 1967, therefore the international community has determined that its permanence in those territories is not valid. Moreover, this Resolution considers it is the biggest obstacle to achieve any peace agreement. Also, is clear the contents of the Resolution 478 about East Jerusalem belonging to the Palestinians but annexed by Israel in 1980, considering it part of its territory. The UN was convinced when said that the Israeli determination, flagrantly violates International law. It is not less clear the Resolution 497 of 1981 that considers the annexation so abusive proclaimed by Israel of the Syrian

By *Kassem Asmar Castellanos*

Golan heights, lacks any validity and legality in the light of the international law. The article 49 of the IV Geneva Convention (Switzerland), also signed by Israel, and where it says that it is forbidden the deportation, transfer and expulsion of people whose territory is under occupation. How many times did Israel violate this Convention since it was signed in 1950?

Photo 2. Source AFP. "A young man raises the Palestinian flag as a sign of rejection of a Jewish settlement that is seen in the background"

Between 2012 and 2013, several investigators appointed by the UN Human Rights Council, conducted a serious research job about the occupied territories, which consisted to investigate and find out the Israeli policy about the illegal settlements in the West Bank. The result of this job leaves no doubt, due to this researcher team concluded that Israel has violated the IV Geneva Convention grossly. The judge Christine Chanet of France, who headed that Commission, said without hesitation that Israel should stop settlements construction unconditionally and begin the dismantling of all settlements in the occupied territories

By Kassem Asmar Castellanos

immediately, including East Jerusalem. This Commission said that Israel applies a policy of aggression and intimidation in order to force the Palestinians to leave their lands for a clear purpose, the expansionism through the policy of building more settlements. The report concludes saying that a Palestinian State without the dismantling the Jewish settlements is not practical.

Once known the outcome, Israel said with a cynical and absurd language, in an entirely ironic way that the policy of settlements in the West Bank is "justified by the Bible". The reader has the last word.

The United States blocked through the use of the veto at the end of 2012, an initiative in the Security Council of the United Nations, condemning the Israeli expansionism with its illegal settlements in the occupied territories. Once again, the United States launches its usual slap against the international legality, supporting the criminal and expansionist activities of its spoiled State of Israel against the Palestinian people.

The situation in the occupied territories, must be understood according the viewpoint of the facts where the perspective shows two cases completely identifiable and differentiable; on the one hand a State whose army is the invader force and that constantly promotes Jewish settlements construction in the West Bank and on the contrary, the Palestinian people who feel how their lives it has become very difficult within their own territory with the Zionist policies of discrimination. It is fair that the Palestinian people demand the Israeli withdrawal from the West Bank. The Palestinian population has to continue defending its legitimate right to the self-determination. Israel must allow, once and for all to Palestinians to live in peace and in freedom as has happened for centuries, before the advent of the Zionist ideology with its perfidious intention to distort what the historical records have proved in their writings, trying to show with fanatical excuses and with a distorted religion saturated with demagogy because of a radical interpretation, in order to convert the illegal practices in legal but at the same time, looking for ingenuous followers citizens through the power of the media prefabricated and distorted.

By Kassem Asmar Castellanos

All of them think as if they were sharing the same mind, same brain, in short a same head where the content of Scripture with a so wildly distorted interpretation and whose results are highly dangerous, because it generates the firm belief that the Jew has the power to act, according to this Zionist contemporary description, as a preferential race and "chosen by the Supreme being". Many renowned rabbis that usually are in Jewish settlements, teaching this dangerous religious doctrine full of bigotry, corroborate this assertion. According to this vision that they have forged, this gives them the right to be "claimants" in each square meter of the surface of the Palestinian territories, but it does not end there if we add the famous and false phrase "a land without people for a people without land", all this seems like a story invented by some famous librettist of Hollywood. Other tactics used by the Zionists in the first decades of the 20th century consisted of displaying publicly, photos of uninhabited places of Palestine in order to "prove" that those lands were uninhabited when the Jews began to arrive in Palestine. Obviously, this kind of tactic is just ridiculous and laughable.

Anyway, the roadmap of these fanatical Jewish settlers is the same, to believe that they have the unmistakable right, not only to occupy lands to build illegal settlements, but also to seize completely their lands. That has been the slogan given by the fundamentalist rabbis. Even they don't hesitate in promoting the use of force as is established by their ideology and biblical teachings as something entirely acceptable. So, the Jewish settlers receive an education full of spiritual intoxication due to religious fanaticism that it impedes to understand the real reason of the conflict, not only in the settlements but also inside Israel.

We all have to agree that this kind of radical indoctrination, whose support is accommodated in the distorted interpretations of the scripture, are supremely harmful because it becomes a barrier of total blindness which is interposed between the rational and Justice and the brutality and injustice on the other hand.

On the basis of this order of ideas, all those Jewish settlements scattered across the occupied territories, represent the hardest obstacle to solve in any dialogue, talks or peace agreement in the Middle East, because of more than 520,000 Jewish colonists who live in settlements in the West Bank and East

By Kassem Asmar Castellanos

Jerusalem, have been indoctrinated in such a way that in their minds, there is not the slightest chance that their settlements can be dismantled. Of course, Israel must assume this responsibility entirely, for having done a systematic policy of colonization in the occupied territories, disrespecting the rules and legality of international law. Therefore, Israel was daring when took the decision of creating this immense problem and his historical role now consists to solve it.

The United States is implicated with this fact because for many years have financed all activities that Israel has implemented in the last 65 years, therefore must accept its high share of responsibility on having supported the expansionism of the State of Israel at the expense of the Palestinian interests.

Without the dismantling of the settlements, a Palestinian State is impossible and unviable because a country cannot develop on disconnected territories. Moreover, economically would not be viable because much of the road network in the occupied West Bank, belongs to the illegal settlements that have permission for its exclusive use and additionally the Jews settlers have special privilege on the water sources of the surface and subsurface of the Palestinian territories. If we consider these realities, in any talk of peace, the problem that represent the settlements should be seen as an enormous obstacle, otherwise it would simply be an insult to the Palestinian people. If the Palestinians accept a State without the dismantling of Jewish settlements, they will dangerously be accepting a destination full of poverty, underdevelopment, and humiliation. This would be an excellent overview for Israel because under this perspective of a Palestinian State surrounded by settlements everywhere, it's really like having a piece of Israel within a Palestinian State and this event can aggravate the spirit of its inhabitants, encouraging the resurgence of violence. Obviously that such a scenery is what always has wanted the occupying forces, to have the pretext and excuse to keep perpetuating its military occupation on the West Bank.

Even political radicals of the Israeli extreme right propose the massive expulsion of Palestinians, because they can go and live in Arab countries, without feeling discriminated. Those Zionists continue with their weak argument that the Arabs have many

By Kassem Asmar Castellanos

Territories, but Israel has a small region. Logically this kind of judgment and proposal, it is an absolute mockery against any average reasoning. Those who have to go away of the Palestinian lands to their respective countries where they were born and grew, are the Jews and not the Palestinians who have lived in this region of the Middle East for many centuries.

A sign that the Palestinians are very affected by the presence of settlements in the occupied territories is the fact that despite, theoretically, Israel withdrew from the Gaza Strip, the situation hasn't changed there. The control of Palestinian groundwater, makes that little of this vital liquid reach that part of Palestine, in addition, the continuous Israeli military and economic siege, are not reasons that the inhabitants of Gaza be happy.

Inexorably, the Palestinians have enough reasons to believe in the non-viability of a Palestinian State, in the middle of many settlers and Jews settlements. This climate of lack of confidence, which has propitiated Israel over several decades with hostile and discriminatory policies against the Palestinians, makes the idea of living among the illegal settlements in the occupied territories, in something impossible from any angle.

Several thinkers have suggested the non-viability of two separate States in the area of conflict, i.e., the Israeli and the Palestinian due to the geographical composition of the occupied territories, on the basis that having so many Jewish settlers and illegal settlements in the West Bank, this precludes to the Palestinians to have an ordinary life, from a social, economic and policy perspective. Therefore, a State under those parameters would make Palestinians live disconnected, in all orders involving an independent nation.

Although the previous argument could be a possibility according to the perspective offered by the current scenario, however the Palestinian stance is much more valid because is convinced that any plan for peace in the region, necessarily must take into account the dismantling of all the settlements, otherwise the Palestinians would end up accepting the Zionist blackmail because they and only they were the architects of the systematic policy of construction of so many Jewish settlements in the occupied territories, then the Palestinians are not obliged to fall in

By Kassem Asmar Castellanos

this game of speculation, previously planned by the occupying forces. We must not forget that from the moment in which they began to build the first settlement in the occupied territories in 1967, all the Arab countries and the international community had declared the illegality of this expansionist policy, and the serious consequences that represented for the future of a solution in the region. Parting from this order of concepts, Israel must assume the responsibility of its disastrous political tactic and not wash its hands, pretending to be the Palestinians who must undertake that Zionist blunder. Even, a part of this guilt of this methodical policy of Israeli expansion in the occupied territories, it has to be assumed by the United States as a power and ally of Israel who didn't do anything to defend the international legality, showing apathy before the continuous violations of Palestinian sovereignty.

Forty-five years later and well into the 21th century, Israel continues building more settlements and at the same time participates in the peace talks with Palestinians with the United States intervention, which occasionally says to Israel with a slight whisper in the ear, "freeze the settlements constructions".

About 150 Jewish settlements in West Bank and East Jerusalem must be added the 32 settlements that were built in the Golan Heights of Syria, rarely mentioned in the peace talks. We have not forget the injustices and aggressions that suffered the Syrian inhabitants of these lands, when were occupied in 1967 by the Israeli army. Many villages were attacked to force more than 95,000 Syrian farmers to leave their homes, and their villages were later destroyed in order to build settlements for the Jewish settlers, in zones free of Syrian presence. The main argument of the Israeli occupation of the Golan Heights is supposedly security for being a high plateau, poses a danger to Israel if it returns to the hands of the Syrians. Today, that argument has lost much weight because Israel considers the Golan Heights of vital importance due to its water sources that supplies water to a significant part of Israel.

Syria never wanted to take part in peace talks because Israel did not want to commitment in the sense of returning the Golan to Syria. Syrian leaders wondered, what is the purpose of the talks proposed by the United States and Israel? The Syrians were always careful with the themes of peace in order to not fall into

By *Kassem Asmar Castellanos*

traps.

The illegal settlements have represented many limitations for the Palestinians when they have to go to work or to their studies centers since they cannot approach to the colonies, even to the roads that are exclusively used by Jewish settlers. Many of the Palestinian farmlands located near settlements were abandoned because the Jewish settlers always are armed, and Palestinian farmers have fear to be received with gunfire. Furthermore, it is quite clear that these attacks stay in total impunity due to the double standards and the racist element, represented in the Israeli judicial system.

Photo 3. Source ALANDETE Jerusalem DAVID 27 FEB 2013-15:58 CET806. MENAHEM KAHANA (AFP). "Image of the construction of a new illegal Jewish settlement in East Jerusalem"

By Kassem Asmar Castellanos

When Israel took the decision to withdraw from the Gaza Strip in 2005 and ordered the dismantling of the settlements that had less than 9,000 Jewish colonists, history cannot deceive the world if it intends to present this fact as a radical shift in Israeli policy toward the Palestinians and peace talks in the Middle East. However the Israeli Prime Minister Ariel Sharon said clearly that it had taken the determination of ordering the dismantling of these settlements for involuntary reasons such as the non-viability that few colonists can stay a longer period, among nearly 1,400,000 Palestinians who lived, in that time, in the Gaza Strip and the severe conditions of its geography. So those who wanted to understand that this withdrawal meant a gesture of good intentions towards the Palestinians, only fell in a high farce, especially that the settlements and the number of Jewish colonists, increased in the West Bank after peace talks with the Palestinians and that was the real gesture of hypocrisy that showed all the time the representatives of the Israeli Government in all the summits.

The media exhibition that was presented by the Israeli Government as a ploy to show the international public opinion the great "sacrifice" that the State of Israel and a few colonists had done, where the settlers were protesting against the "historical determination" of Ariel Sharon. This theatrical performance caused indignation and rage among connoisseurs, especially the Palestinians. So shameful was the spectacle that exposed the different media of Israel; the withdrawal of the settlers with cries of hysteria and hurling slogans against the Government of Israel that can only be compared with the great humanitarian tragedies that the Palestinians have lived. Obviously the big difference that continues being extremely abysmal, is that the tragedies of displacement and expulsions of Palestinians had involved more than 1.2 million Palestinians and not the 8,500 Jewish colonists who were illegally established in the Gaza Strip.

Israel has a long theatrical career, showing himself as a victim instead of its real facade, which is the perpetrator. The Zionist movements in Europe and the United States have made a harmful performance, working against the interests of the Palestinian people since that fateful day of meeting at the Basel Congress in Switzerland, who their greatest leader Theodor Herzel convened at the end of the 19th century, whose "axiom"

By Kassem Asmar Castellanos

backed by a "Divine Mandate" gave the right to the Zionist Jews to colonize every corner of Palestine. Those Zionist organizations that have accomplished for more than one century the murky task of promoting the colonization of the Palestinian territories. Obviously, they had particular collaboration from Israel, after the founding of the Jewish State in 1948. In fact, this partnership well into the 21th century remains as faithful as in the beginning.

It is pertinent to indicate that the cheeky and systematic policy of Israel, it reached very worrisome levels for the Palestinians, as soon were occupied the territories of West Bank, Gaza and the Golan Heights in 1967. Although Israel had occupied the Sinai of Egypt, this last territory did not offer interesting things, since it was a desert in North Africa where Israel couldn't get good benefits, in contrast to the other occupied territories whose main interest for Israel are its fertile lands and water sources.

To avoid that Jewish colonists fall in monotony and lack of interest in the settlements where they live in the occupied territories, the Zionist State started to give them what most of intermediate European cities have, such as: swimming pools, supermarkets, pharmacies, shops, cinemas, kindergartens, schools, among others. Even, many of those settlements have factories that produce different kinds of articles. Anyway, the idea of authorities of Israel and the World Zionist Organization was that they had to consent the Jewish colonists in order to avoid the possible return to their homes and countries of origin where they should actually live and not in the Palestinian territories. For settlers who come from outside, everything it becomes easier since the Israeli Government provides them with cheap housings, subsidized studies, work guaranteed with good salary and comforts. Everything was coldly calculated to encourage Jews migration from Europe and America to the occupied territories.

Nor should we ignore the harsh reality that all the rulers of Israel are guided by a Zionist ideology with racist tendency and Apartheid policies in the occupied territories. Since Israel was founded in 1948 with David Ben Gurion as Prime Minister who was seconded by Golda Meir, Isaac Rabin, Shimon Peres, Menachem Begin, Yitzhak Shamir, Benjamin Netanyahu, Ehud Barak, Ariel Sharon, Ehud Olmert. All these rulers, exercised their functions, taking as base the Zionist ideology of expansionism on

By Kassem Asmar Castellanos

the Palestinian territories.

In order to understand this issue, unlike what happened in South Africa where the black population was well discriminated by the racist Government and Apartheid system in South Africa, assigning them the worst jobs, wages, schools and education, beaches, restaurants, housing, medical care and everything that encloses everyday life of a society, but those leaders never had intention to expel them, although this fact doesn´t minimizes the historic responsibility of these rulers who applied policies of racial segregation which meant a shameful exploitation and humiliation of the black population in South Africa. It is significant to clarify that the Israeli Zionist Government, it is sustained by harmful ideologies even worse than those that were applied in South Africa, because the rules that apply in the occupied territories are clearly very discriminatory against Palestinians but there is a practice that it didn´t reach South Africa, and it is the expulsion and displacement of more than 1,200,000 Palestinians since Israel creation.

Previously, it was mentioned that the World Zionist movement, had always used the religion and the ancient Holy Scriptures as a pretext to assault the Palestinian territories, therefore the relationship that maintains so close each other, the World Zionist Organization and the State of Israel, is based that both of them are inherent and functional in the own Zionism ideology and has always kept this structure, before and after the creation of the State of Israel. If we analyze the policy of Israel in the occupied territories, we see that there is no difference between the vision and mission of the World Zionist movement. Both the State of Israel and the World Zionist movement preach the same objectives as is the increase of the Jewish settlements in the occupied territories, the Jews migration from different parts to the Palestinian territories, to foster agricultural activities to ensure more expropriation of Palestinian lands, subsidy and permanent support to Jewish colonists to make sure its permanence in the occupied territories and settlements, the cultural and religious indoctrination of the Jewish migrants to convince them of their "historic rights that have by divine mandate" in the West Bank, Gaza and in whole Jerusalem, among other goals.

By Kassem Asmar Castellanos

There are several essays and documents relating to Jewish settlements in the West Bank, where it is manifested that a country or independent nation for Palestinians is practically unfeasible because of, there are many scattered settlements through the four cardinal points in the occupied territories, so the task of its dismantlement is almost impossible.

All the Palestinians agree with the non-viability of a Palestinian State in the middle of this vast settlement network, by the reasons and explanations that were shown in several sections in this book. What the Palestinians don't accept is the weak argument that these settlements may not be dismantled. The idea of dismantling should be understood by the side of the relocation within Israel, of Jewish colonists who live now in those settlements. The issue of settlements must be seen as physical infrastructure that can even be purchased by the oil countries of this region and these in turn, become funds of compensation in a hopeful future for settlers that it could mean they should leave the settlements in an eventual Israeli-Palestinian peace agreement. In this way, both Jewish settlers and Palestinians would benefit and much more the same peace process that could reach a definitive solution for both sides. Another argument less valid would be that Israel shows its endless expansionist countenance, pretending to reach a final peace agreement with the Palestinians, while retaining the settlements in the occupied territories. As once a Palestinian leader said, referring to the Israeli position "I want the peace but the Palestinian territories too "

In conclusion, peace in the Middle East, and more specifically in the occupied territories, it depends punctually on the degree of commitment and seriousness that Israel should assume. So, the Palestinians have to stay firm in the sense that they have not to allow the permanence of settlements in the occupied territories, isn't it enough 78% of Palestinian territory where rests the current state of Israel? The Palestinians are only claiming 22% of all the Palestinian territories that until 1947 belonged to them entirely. There is no moral justification, for not withdrawing from the occupied territories and also to order the withdrawal of Jewish colonists that the same Israel, helped to place in the West Bank.

By Kassem Asmar Castellanos

In the hypothetical event of a Palestinian State with the conditions of Jewish settlements without significant changes, how would the distribution of the water be?, who would set the rates for water and electricity for Palestinians?, how and under what conditions could move the Palestinians to their jobs, study, among others?, how would be the labor and economic connections among the Palestinian cities that are at the moment, as a kind of fragmented cantons?, what would be the conditions that permit the farmers send their products to the different markets? What will happen with the lands that Jewish settlers have cultivated, but that were improperly evicted from the hands of Palestinian farmers by the Israeli occupying forces? These and other questions that the Palestinians should analyze carefully before signing any peace agreement in order to avoid unpleasant surprises that could mean a very hard blow to the Palestinian claims.

Another critical point in a future Israeli-Palestinian peace agreement is the immediate dismantling and destruction of the separation wall that has meant a fatal injury to Palestinians. In fact, it must be destroyed since with its route, Israel has appropriated part of the West Bank that remains under occupation since 1967.

The Israeli argument not so convincing, that the conflict between Palestinians and Israelis would have been avoided if the Arabs had accepted the partition plan proposed by the UN in 1947. This argument has no historical basis according the circumstances and conditions contained in this scheme. Do not forget that in the context, in which this proposal was developed, Great Britain had participated actively, encouraging Jewish migration to Palestine, also the weapons that permanently acquired from British and this support was openly referenced through the Balfour Declaration in 1917. In that same year, the Jews didn't pass of 65,000 inhabitants, while the Palestinians were 630,000, i.e. it was a ratio of one to ten, but in 1947 when the Palestine partition was proposed, according how it was planned by Western powers that wanted to show a "friendly gesture" with the Zionist movements. This plan had been developed it in such way that it was evident that they were favoring the Jews, but in spite of the continuous migrations that for so many years, several European countries had sponsored such

By Kassem Asmar Castellanos

as Great Britain, the majority of population in Palestine were Palestinians. On the eve of the starting the discussions in the General Assembly of the United Nations, there were 1,220,000 Palestinian inhabitants and 600,000 Jews and this dramatic change in the demographic composition in Palestine, has its explanation in the exaggerated Jewish migrations, sponsored by the World Zionist movement, however, while the Palestinians were much more than the Jewish inhabitants, the shameful partition gave 56% of Palestine to Jews who were a minority, including the best agricultural lands . Weren´t they enough reasons for rejecting this unjust plan for the interests of the Palestinian people?

When Israel talks about this specific topic brings to public light a farce in the sense that the Arabs rejected that plan because its goal was to destroy Israel and expel the Jews. This is not true, this Zionist strategy reflects a clear intention of misleading the world public opinion because the facts have proved the opposite conclusion since those who were expelled, abused and their lands confiscated, have been Palestinians throughout the 20th century and 21th. Conclusion, Israel has sought to reverse the order of the equation, insinuating that is the victim of the conflict rather than the actual role that has fulfilled: the perpetrator.

Several European countries have begun to understand the importance of not following the Israeli game with its intention to legitimize the illegal Jewish settlements in the occupied territories, in the sense that the agricultural products, produced by Jewish settlers in the occupied regions of the West Bank, the Golan Heights and East Jerusalem, which are subsequently exported to a part of Europe in countries such as Ireland, the Netherlands, Denmark and the United Kingdom. Due to the fact that these products carry a small label that says "Made in Israel", and as a result of this illegal practice, these countries have come to the conclusion that those articles are produced in the occupied territories and not in Israel, so they must not have that misleading label. Additionally, since 1967 the international community considers illegal the settlers who live in settlements in the heart of the occupied territories. Similarly, most countries belonging to the European Union have adopted the same measure, in order to not support the grotesque Israeli maneuver.

By Kassem Asmar Castellanos

The Palestinians have expressed their intention of living, side by side, with the Israelis with the condition that any peace proposal, it should take into account their rights, i.e., no more tricks and no more deceptions.

4. ISRAEL AND PALESTINE FROM THE ANALYTICAL VIEWPOINT OF THE MOST DISTINGUISHED REVISIONISTS

To avoid confusion or misinterpretations, it must be clarified that although all Zionists are Jews, not all Jews are Zionists. There are a lot of Jews from different parts of the world, even within Israel who never agreed with the expansionist policies and the racist measures that promulgate the Zionism. Among these groups, there are prominent Jews who have known to win the respect and recognition from an important sector of the international community.

The famous Nobel Prize winner for physics Albert Einstein, who professed the Jewish religion, had rejected the invitation that certain Zionist organizations sent him in order to join the global Zionist project. What the Zionist leaders didn't know is that Einstein had gotten enough information about the events that were developing in Palestine and of the atrocities that were being perpetrated against the Palestinian people and where he blamed the British and the Zionist movements of all these injustices. The famous Nobel Prize winner never doubted to categorize to all these Zionist groups as terrorist organizations whose mission was to sow panic in Palestine to get that cruel goal at the expense of the Palestinians.

In Israel and elsewhere in the world, have appeared several scholars and historians who have placed much emphasis on deepening through an investigative analysis in the historical study from the new contributions that have appeared on the events that preceded the creation of the State of Israel and its subsequent expansionism. These academics and Jewish researchers who took the decision to explore the truth, are considered as historical revisionists. Those experts academics, tired of the endless inconsistencies and deceptions about the process that preceded the establishment of Jewish migrants and its subsequent scattering of settlements throughout Palestine, wanted to show their point of view as result of the conclusions that contributed their research whose aim has been to the approaching to the truth of these historical facts.

By Kassem Asmar Castellanos

To avoid suspicions, it is essential to point out that the position of these academic figures and historians was not influenced by anybody, but by their exhaustive investigative jobs of a large number of sources and historical documents.

Below, it will be exposed a brief summary of the thought of some of these revisionists on the topic which contains in particular, the Israeli-Palestinian conflict:

Moshe Zimmermann is a Professor of the Hebrew University in Jerusalem. He says that voluntary Jewish soldiers, who want to serve especially in the occupied territories, are like the Germans voluntarily, who wanted to be part of the dreaded SS. Continues saying that the young settlers in Hebron who are trained radically, are compared with the Hitler youth.

He has no doubt that the Holocaust was exploited to the maximum by the Zionists to be able to convince the imperialist powers of the need for the creation of a State for the Jews in Palestine and not hesitate by saying that Hitler deserves a special gratitude, for having created the Holocaust that helped the Zionist project. It must be clarified that Moshe Zimmermann like the rest of the world, flatly rejected the insane attitude of Nazism against the Jews, but additionally, he rejects the Zionist's tactic in the sense of taking advantage from a historical fact, that was a catastrophe for the Jewish people in Europa in order to justify criminal acts and injustice measures against a people who had lived in that region for centuries and who was deprived of all their rights, as what happened to the Palestinian population. Zimmermann continues with his analysis, saying that this kind of education that is taught to the Jewish colonist children in Hebron, is so radical that make them feel a superior race and that the Palestinians are simply enemies, also shows that there are politicians in high-profile who insinuate the importance of the expulsion of all Palestinians from the occupied territories, so we can set a comparative parallel with the planned by Hitler to expel all Jews from Germany.

Even, Professor Zimmermann publicly denounces, the intention of the Israeli authorities to expel them and other historians and academic revisionists for not sharing the Zionist ideology. Wasn't that the Hitler method with those who didn't want to obey the Nazi thinking?

72

By Kassem Asmar Castellanos

This renowned Professor does not hide his disappointment when considers a blunder, the apathetic position of an important part of the Israeli society, on the search of a true agreement peace with the Palestinians. He does not conceive the possibility of a Palestinian State, surrounded by Jewish settlements everywhere, simply because it lacks common sense.

He highlights something interesting that can benefit the both people in the future, once created the Palestinian State, a bilateral economic cooperation. But while radical right political leaders continue with the thesis that all Palestine is a part of Israel then, what is going to be discussed in a process of peace with the Palestinians? There is a clear and marked contradiction between the search for peace and the real intentions of Israel.

Avi Shlaim is an Israeli historian who has studied the foundations of the Jewish State even before its creation. Author of an interesting book "the wall of iron, Israel, and the Arab world". After an exhaustive investigation, he affirms that the intentions of Zionism was to use only a plan supported by a racist ideology as a mechanism to seize the whole of Palestine, as it seems in the speeches of the main Zionist leaders in the first part of the 20th century. To reaffirm that plan, they had to create a powerful army to ensure such expansionism.

Avi Shlaim like other academic revisionists, insists that while the problem of settlements is not resolved in the occupied territories, it cannot reach a peace agreement with the Palestinians, therefore the problem of the stagnation of the peace process, is due to Israeli policy that does not show interest to achieve such goal, and if shows it, is simply an hypocritical posture to gain time and to present an image to the world that Israel wants peace. Moreover, Avi Shlaim ensures that Israel takes political and military decisions regardless how delicate are, without consulting anyone.

This Israeli author makes a valid reflection wondering until when, Israel should keep its emotional state on high alert against its Arab neighbors, with a State permanently militarized with a giant army, compared with the demographic dimension that it has.

73

By *Kassem Asmar Castellanos*

On the other hand, the Israeli historian Shlomo Sand well versed in specific issues such as the creation of Israel and a history professor at a recognized University in Tel Aviv, author of several books about the creation of Israel and the role of Zionism to achieve this end. He has many reasons to doubt about the Zionist thesis of lineage and descent Jewish, as the Zionist leaders present it since their first speech at the beginning of the 20th century. Shlomo Sand ensures that most of the Jews who lived outside Palestine, had belonged to regions who had no religion and later were converted to Judaism and the thesis of the Zionist organizations, it can't be true in the sense that the Jews are descendants of ancient Jews. This author reached to disturb the tranquility of many Zionists when after a serious investigative study, said that the only descendants of ancient Jews are the Arab-Palestinians.

He is clear and forceful when affirms that the Zionism in the 19th century, devised the concept of a Jewish people based in religious interpretations as a great invention in order to be able to justify the need for a homeland in Palestine. With that set of ideas, Shlomo Sand says that even the French could not ensure that several centuries ago, there were French people. Similarly happens with the Jews where most of them, are Jews by conversion from a recent period of history, so they don't have a common origin. He even makes a very important revelation saying that prominent Jewish leaders that were symbols of the Zionist thesis, like David Ben Gurion and Yitzhak Ben Zvi, had written at the start of the 20th century that authentic descendants of the Jews are Arab Palestinians. Obviously, that conclusion it could not keep up to the order of the public opinion in general, especially because it was already brewing the Zionist plan in order to take over Palestine and that it could be transformed in an apparent contradiction, therefore it was decided to archive the thesis at the end of the twenties of the 20th century.

This historian says the great fraud and manipulation that the Zionists made on this topic consist that they don't present Jewish religion as such, but as a people and nation. Zionist logic of its thesis is that any Jew either German, French, Italian, Hungarian, Polish, Russian, etc., can automatically after a minimum requirement, be an Israeli citizen. In fact that Israel is a compendium of Jews from many countries of the world. So the same content of the Declaration of Israel reeling when he said that Israel was the birthplace of the Jewish people and of their spiritual, religious, political and cultural formation, How it can be emphasized with that statement when most Jews are converts and from other places as Europe? Shlomo Sand is author of several books, but which resulted in more emotional followers and detractors it's titled "the invention of the Jewish people".

Shlomo Sand confirms what other historians had suspected and affirmed in the sense that Zionism took sections of biblical texts and made it official history to give a valid seal to its thesis the "promised land" in order to take over Palestine, pretending to prove that it belongs to the Jewish people. He called Zionists of being a fundamentalist movement showing themselves as a movement of political ideology, but ultimately what they did was take advantage of biblical myths with the objective of turning them into official history with a national geopolitical purpose.

Shlomo mentions that for the sake of peace and justice, Israel should be behind the 1967 borders and give free rein to the Palestinians for their independence since Israel is an occupying force in West Bank. He concludes by saying that Jews are descendants of crossbreeding links and only through the shameless falsification of history, they have tried to show them as a people with their own identity and culture and ancestral allegiance to a religious tradition. Those who have contributed most with that falsification and manipulation of history were the Zionists of late 19th century and early 20th.

Ilan Pappe does not need presentation since this revisionist and Israeli historian, is a valid point of reference to understand the Palestinian cause in its purest dimension. About the creation of Israel and the events that surrounded it before and after 1948, Pappe does not hesitate to point out that it applied a process of ethnic cleansing against the Palestinian people, to impose Jewish presence at any human cost. The result of those systematic crimes sponsored by world Zionism is reflected in the destruction of hundreds of villages, the murder of many defenseless civilians and the expulsion by force of thousands of Palestinians.

By Kassem Asmar Castellanos

Ilan Pappe was for a long time professor at the Hebrew University of Haifa and author of several books on the subject that surrounds the Israeli-Palestinian conflict. There is no way to blame this author and academic of speculator since part of his source to reach the conclusion that there was ethnic cleansing against the Palestinians, are documents that were recently declassified and that corroborates what many Arab researchers had written over the last 60 years. This time, the same comment is especially important because it was written by Jewish authors and Israeli academics who reject categorically the grotesque and blatant fallacies of the Zionists when they say that Al-Nakba was a voluntary departure of the Palestinians, due to the advice of several Arab leaders, also according to these same Zionists, the destruction of hundreds of villages, didn't happen.

The investigative job of Pappe, finished confirming that there were expulsions in large quantities, through violent and armed coercion that caused criminal Zionist groups. This author ensures that the Zionist movement, in the early 20th century, invented and orchestrated a booklet dotted with lies and deception in order to convince world public opinion that they were seriously planning to create a homeland for the Jews in "uninhabited lands"

Pappe exposes in his famous book "the Palestinian ethnic cleansing", that a short time before beginning the discussions about approval for the creation of the State of Israel, Ben Gurion was doing mischief in some corner of Tel Aviv, when devised with other Zionists, the notorious Plan Dalet, which at that time had approximately in its ranks more than 50,000 well-armed men, where a considerable part of them had participated and trained with the British forces during the second world war. Dalet plan suggested putting up a violent practice as a mechanism to depopulate the villages and small Palestinian cities, in order to inhabit them with Jewish immigrants and thus, distort the geographical and demographic features and the own history of the Palestinian territories. The fundamental objective of Dalet Plan was that Palestine had to be a unique home for the Jews. Despite the fact that in 1947 they were little more than a third of the population and they did not have more than 8% of the Palestinian territories, blatantly, the UN commanded by the United States had assigned to the Jews, 56% of Palestine and as if that was not enough, at the end of 1948 Zionism began already to control 78% of Palestine.

Ilan Pappé said that al-Nakba didn't finish in 1948 because in 1967, although on a smaller scale, the drama was repeated when military authorities of Israel forced many Palestinians to leave their lands, especially by imposing stifling laws to break the will of the Palestinian people, since were promulgated laws as excuse in order to make arrests without charges or trials. The Zionist State, also made abusive practices as the demolitions of Palestinian homes, with the aim to Judaize militarily the occupied territories (to turn many areas of the West Bank, in places immensely populated with Jews, changing its appearance demographic, cultural, historical and geographical). This kind of abuse continues until today.

This author says that, although the Palestinian uprising against Israeli occupation known as the Intifada, has attracted an important solidarity in the world public opinion, it has not been sufficient to put an end to decades of occupation. However, the voices of condemnation of the Israeli occupation have grown in recent years but it should continue working in that direction in order to change the situation into concrete action through effective policies that have some impact on the policy of Israeli occupation.

Pappe says there is no freedom of speech in Israel due to the censorship, especially when someone tries into question, the policy of Israeli occupation. In this aspect, the treatment that the Palestinians receive is much harder than those that Israeli citizens receive. For example, in the case of Ilan Pappe who has denounced the Israeli occupation policies and abuse which the Palestinian people have suffered, due to the suffocating military rules imposed by Israel, even, it made Pappe lose his job and has also been discriminated, because he was considered anti-Jewish and anti-Semite for having dared to show the truth. But if a Palestinian does that kind of statements, he could be arrested and mistreated.

By Kassem Asmar Castellanos

According to this famous Israeli revisionist, Israeli citizens don't know the reality of the occupied territories because have not been personally there and they only dispose of manipulated information of the Zionist authorities. Even the Jewish colonists who are living inside the West Bank settlements, don't know reality thoroughly, because they think that the Palestinians have a normal life without any setback.

The author emphasizes the importance of implementing campaigns of boycott and other sanctions against Israel that go along with the Organization of non-violent resistance in Palestine. In 2010 at a Conference in the German city of Stuttgart, Pappe said since before 1948, the intention of Zionism has been to destroy the lives of the Palestinians and since then its policies have not changed, because while try to show some facets about the peace negotiations, they continue simultaneously trampling Palestinian rights. This academic has no doubt that what the Zionism had done in 1948, was an ethnic cleansing against the Palestinians. Additionally, he reveals that Israeli soldiers were trained ideologically in such a way, in order to see the Palestinians as enemies. So the worst enemy of the Palestinians is the racist system of the Israeli State that imposes a fascist ideology that generates hatred and violence.

The shameful action that ended involving the United Nations in 1948 which had the "approval" of part of the international community with the slogan of Justice and peace consisted in that the UN allowed the expulsion of more than half of the Palestinian population, because it allegedly sought a just and peaceful solution in Palestine, therefore the same application and idea that it focused on the partition of Palestine is immoral and unfortunately the Palestinian ethnic cleansing, took place under the light of the international support, allowing the implementation of the Zionist projects. Pappe wonders is this a legitimate way of doing democracy, saying that it is the only one in the Middle East? The big lie that Israel intends to maintain is when says that Israel is the only place where Jews can reemerge as a national movement and exercise their right of self- determination. The intention of this Zionist claim, has a clear target which is to encourage the migration and the Jewish colonization of the occupied territories.

By Kassem Asmar Castellanos

That author reaffirms some changes in the pronouncements of several Western Governments in condemning, in a theoretical principle, to Israel for its policies of occupation, but the problem is that the words alone won't change the situation of the Palestinians, as indeed it has not changed in the last 65 years and this it can be seen when Israel ignores these criticisms, so it is necessary to impose serious sanctions against the occupation forces, in order to oblige Israel to review its policies in this part of the Middle East, otherwise, very little will change. The main problem continues being the huge military, economic and diplomatic support, that Israel receives from the United States and this ends up making to Zionist State more intransigent and arrogant because they feel confident and strong with the American support.

Many aspects of the serious and investigative work of Ilan Pappe are plausible, although we have a somewhat distant appreciation in relation to see a possible self-determination of the Palestinian people with an own State, due to that Pappe is absolutely convinced that two States, cannot be given in this specific region. Pappe thinks the best solution is one single State for the both people, in which take into account the democratic precepts, also, justice must be provided equally for all and the identities and rights of all are respected.

Although this approach of a single State for the two peoples, i.e., for the Palestinians and the Israelis, it would be ideal, but in practice I think it would be the total annihilation of the Palestinian people, due to the Machiavellian plans and strategies that the Zionists had devised more than 110 years ago, of a Jewish State in Palestine, it conceived this as a religious-ethnic State, based on a racist and dominant ideology where manipulated at their will, the ancient biblical Scripture in order to justify the theft of lands from the Palestinians with the laughable and ludicrous argument of "a land without people for a people without land", with a systematic expansionist tactics, which consisted of expelling Palestinians through the use of all available means and almost simultaneously, being replaced by Jewish immigrants. Indeed, it is not surprising that today there are so many Jewish settlements in the occupied territories in the West Bank that is home to hundreds of thousands of Jewish colonists armed with assault rifles to protect themselves from their "Palestinian enemies". Therefore, watching the expansionist Israeli appetite and its mental mechanization through a Zionist pedagogy from classrooms, combined with an exaggerated propaganda to show the Jew as superior race, due to a "divine will" that interpret as their right over these lands, I doubt that the Zionists and Israelis want that kind of national symbiosis.

For that kind of approach, there must be a social and cultural transformation towards a sincere pedagogy, honest and with a moral content to know the contemporary history and the truth that surrounded the events and thus purify the hearts of all those who live in that ancient land. The first step it should be given, to understand the suggestion of Pappe, is that the scars must heal and then contemplate the possibility of a single State. I am afraid that the issue isn't at all an easy task. On the other hand, the Israelis always showed little interest in fixing the outstanding matters because the passage of time favors them. The most obvious indication that Israel does not want the peace, was the rejection of the plan which Saudi Arabia put to consideration of the international community and the Arab League at the beginning of 2002, Days after, the European Union and the Arab League showed their approval but Israel immediately rejected it. The content of this initiative could not be more ambitious, since the Arab countries showed willingness to take a step forward about something that in the past would have been almost impossible. The main Point of this peace proposal is that all Arab countries would be willing to normalize relations with Israel in all fields; in exchange Israel has to withdraw from the occupied territories to the lines as they were drawn, immediately before the 1967 war. The above according to the Resolutions of the United Nations.

We return to the same point because Israel wants the Palestinian representatives accept a kind of peace plan with trap against the Palestinian people, that consists the Zionist State reaches the peace, but at the same time to continue keeping its presence in the West Bank and on the basis of that order of concepts, it is virtually impossible that the Arabs and Palestinians are ready to sign this kind of initiative or proposal which is not serious. So, the problem is not with the Palestinians but with the Israeli State that doesn't want to comply with the legal system that the international community has established. Another great reason that puts into question the feasibility of a single State for both people is the fact that the authorities of Israel come with an argument not so old, related with the settlements in the sense that now, they have the insolence to say that Israel has the right to enlarge its settlements in the West Bank, due to "natural expansion". For example, if a settlement has 3,000 Jewish colonists but with the passing of time, they are more, could be 4,000 or 5,000 colonists in an hypothetical case. On the basis of this new demographic perspective, the Israeli authorities assume their own right of its particular interpretation, by saying that it is legal the annexation of more Palestinian territories to respond to this "natural expansion" and if this is little, to increase the looting from the West Bank underground water.

In addition, how it will call this State? Palestinian-Israeli? Who would rule in the ministries and political aspects? How would be formed a possible shared Parliament? How resources such as water, electricity, road network and fertile lands would be used? i.e., Would everyone have the same right? What would be the status of Jewish settlements in the West Bank? And so many questions that make the idea of a single State for both peoples be something utopian.

The problem with a single State are not Palestinians, but the same Zionist ideological conception which invalidates any participation of the Arab-Palestinians, since this ideology believes that the only ones who have the right over all the Palestinian territory, are Jews no matter where they come from.

Noam Chomsky, great philosopher and American analyst of Jewish origin, Is one of the most significant thinker of recent decades and has been mentioned in this work for two reasons, first because together with Ilan Pappe has done a great investigative contribution on the topic, which involves the Israeli-Palestinian problem and the occupied territories and the second reason is that he is a great visionary with special credibility, who is respected in many countries around the world, to expose his views about the U.S. foreign policy in all areas and facts surrounding several regions of the planet.

By Kassem Asmar Castellanos

Once I was doing a dissertation in one Colombian University about this topic and I remember during this speech, I was interrupted suddenly by a small group of students, when I said the best excuse that Israel has, to continue using its expansionist tactic and criminal aggression over occupied Palestinian territories, is precisely that Hammas continue firing their Qassam rockets towards Israel, since their effects are minor damages on the ground and the outbreak of glass in buildings and with this, no one should justify those actions, however, the grossly disproportionate response of the Israeli army, which result is a massive destruction in lives and in infrastructure to Palestine civilians with its powerful air and land arsenal, it must be condemned. The latest raids and offensives of the Israeli army in the Gaza Strip as a response to releases of Qassam rockets by militias of Hamas could be summarized in the following manner: at late 2008 and early 2009, Israel activated its warmongering plan against Gaza, plan known as "cast lead". To tell the truth, who ended worse than those words because of that cowardly action and barbarity, were the unarmed Palestinian civilians, since the result of that criminal incursion by land and air with relentless bombing, could not be different; 1350 Palestinians dead (defenseless civilians mostly) and 17 Israelis dead where most of them were military. Even the building of the United Nations in Gaza, didn´t escape from the bombings.

It is not difficult to conclude that there were never clashes between opposite armed forces, but an unilateral savage and cruel attack by air and land, against the defenseless people of Gaza.

Although to a lesser extent, in November 2012 was repeated the Israeli criminal performance when revived its military offensive against the Gaza Strip, this time named "defensive pillar" and as usual, the result was 140 Palestinians dead, the vast majority civilians. In Israel, there were no victims except a few wounded who could be counted with the hands fingers. If we add the two Zionist criminal offensives on Gaza, the result is 1,490 Palestinians killed and only 17 Israelis dead. The result is very eloquent because Israel practices a criminal policy against the Palestinians, similar to a lawless bandit.

By Kassem Asmar Castellanos

The reflection and conclusion that we have to do is, what favor does Hamas do to the Palestinians when continue launching their rockets, knowing that the Israeli response against the Palestinians is more than genocide? Palestinians have only one way of fighting and is through demonstrations and peaceful protest and obviously, disclosing to the international public opinion the injustices that are happening in the occupied territories, otherwise, it would be a fight between a tiger and a tied person.

About this topic, I am comforted to read a few notes contained in an interview, that Noam Chomsky granted to Frank Barat, renowned journalist and human rights activist where Chomsky says, that the Israeli State and its rulers, always end up favored with the launching of Qassam rockets by Hamas. This gives the perfect excuse to Israel to respond with the maximum violence to that "Palestinian terrorist" aggression and cause many deaths and destruction among the Palestinians. Therefore for Israel it is the best gift, that Hamas continues throwing their Qassam Rockets. Chomsky carries on saying: the best thing that the Palestinians can do is to assume a fight without violence, trough protests and demonstrations that is where success can be achieved.

It would be an irreverence to disregard the name of Norman Finkelstein, since is an authority of great analytical projection with a very accepted credibility, at the moment of exposing his ideas about the problems in the occupied territories. Of Jewish parents who had face desperately, the Nazi persecution. Although he is not an Israeli citizen, this American knows better than anyone else, all circumstances that surrounded the creation of the State of Israel and the penury that the Palestinian people had to live, under the occupation of the Hebrew State forces in recent decades. His mother, a woman with unbreakable and faultless morality, always instilled in the young Finkelstein, the appreciation towards moral and truth above any consideration or subjective palpitations. For this reason, it is an honor to have the opportunity to mention him in this simple work, in order to learn from his academic research experiences and thus to find a clear light at the end of the tunnel.

By Kassem Asmar Castellanos

In his book "The Holocaust Industry", Finkelstein begins discovering the manipulation that the Zionist movements had given to the question of the Holocaust, as a showcase to justify their actions after the end of World War II, with the addition of many sympathizers from everywhere, due to the image of the Holocaust and the concentration camps.

He has no doubt that the image of the Holocaust has been exploited by Israel until the present day to carry out any kind of military action, not only against Palestinians, but also against its Arab neighbors.

Finkelstein says that the popularity toward Israel came into a free fall after the 1967 war, since once the war was over, world public opinion began to hear about abuses that the occupying forces were applying against the Arab-Palestinians and the treatment so inhuman that the Palestinians suffered, in order to force them to leave their lands. The international support to Israel reached its lowest level. Finkelstein says that the image of Israel fell so much that the Zionist ringleaders and the Jewish lobby in the United States activated a plan to seek, again, the solidarity of international opinion but always taking advantage of the cruel image of the Jewish suffering during the Holocaust in the hands of the Nazis. So, Finkelstein explains that Israel since its establishment, always has committed crimes and outrages, hiding behind what the world knew about the Holocaust, presenting the Zionists as victims of any action, i.e., passing of perpetrators to victims, trying to justify any criminal action against Palestinians.

This author insists on saying that Israel committed many abuses in Palestine as for example the mass expulsion of Palestinians to be able, systematically, steal their lands in order to be distributed to the Jewish immigrants, who came to Palestine from different parts of the world, but Finkelstein continues explaining that the Israeli and Zionist impertinence consisted in taking advantage of the harsh images of the Holocaust with lies and deception advertising, presenting Israel as the victim who always is being violently besieged by its Arab neighbors. Different media are mostly under the control of Jews; therefore they exaggerate, accommodate and misrepresent the information in favor of Israel.

In another aspect, and in this agree the majority who have had the opportunity of studying and reviewing the course of events and the historical developments in Palestine since the beginning of the 20th century until the present day, Finkelstein unravels the false idea, when the Zionist Israelis and American politicians have tried to present the Israeli- Palestinian conflict as a matter of very complex to solve and therefore it will take much time for a definitive solution. Well, that is totally false. The Palestinian issue has not been resolved because Americans and Israelis don´t have political intention in this sense and less moral attitude. Israel does not want to join to the legality of the international community, refusing to withdraw its occupying forces and settlements from the West Bank and that is precisely what makes the Palestinian conflict be so complex, not by part of the Palestinians but by the obstacles that has been imposing the Israeli State over decades.

Unfortunately, this situation has been maintained due to the constant blockade that United States has exercised with the use of the veto to stop any initiative that is presented by the international community, in the main precinct of the United Nations Security Council. So, the right of the Palestinian people has no much relevance for the United States, since the great country of the north only shows interest, in safeguarding the illegitimate interests of Israel in the occupied territories. Therefore, is giving his back to the law and international principles.

Jimmy Carter appears in this segment of the book for several reasons, but the most important, because he was President of the United States from 1977 to 1981, but the most important reason that prompted me to mention him, is that Carter was one of the U.S. Presidents who gave more military and economic support to Israel throughout his Government, but years later and far from political life and with the help of a more favorable climate for reflection, notoriously changed his vision about the conflict between Palestinians and Israelis. How could this happen? Very easy, we should not convert that change into an event of the size of China´s wall. The answer is that this former president had spent enough time to study and research the contemporary history of Palestine and came to the conclusion that all the facts that surrounded the creation of the State of Israel and the expansionism carried out by this State to control the whole of

By Kassem Asmar Castellanos

Palestine, it was simply held to a spiral of deceit, lies and misrepresentation of the real and true events by the same authorities of Israel and the Zionist movements.

Because of the publication of his book: "Palestine: peace and not Apartheid", Carter dared to denounce publicly with this work, the semi-covert truth of the aggressive and racist policies of Israel against the Palestinians. His book has taken much more relevance due to that the author is a respected figure and became the first former President in daring to speak bluntly, about the Palestinian issue.

Jimmy Carter concludes and corroborates with a direct language that the stagnation of the peace process between Israelis and Palestinians is due to permanent obstacles that Israel shows to prevent reach a serious agreement with the Palestinians, in that sense the intransigence of the Israeli leaders, says Carter, is clear because they don't want to obey the International laws. Not only are reluctant to a withdrawal from occupied territories, but also they continue practicing, against the Palestinians, a policy of oppression and racist measures.

Another serious obstacle is the constant American support to Israel and obviously it is notorious that the United States makes little effort to solve this conflict. This makes the anti-American sentiment around the world, increases because they see that American leaders tolerate all the human rights violations against the Palestinians with much complacency.

For example Carter speaks about the enormous wall built by Israel, with the excuse that it is to ensure security to Israeli citizens. Well, the real purpose of this wall is to continue appropriating of what little is left of Palestinian lands, because clearly it enters into the West Bank and additionally to that, to maintain safe the Jewish colonists who live in settlements that are illegally in the occupied territories. Carter accuses Israel of implementing a policy of State that consists in discrimination, abuse and the use of force, and the institutionalization of the dispossession policy, and land confiscation to colonize as much as possible, the occupied territories of the West Bank.

By Kassem Asmar Castellanos

The epithet Apartheid that Carter has been using when refers to Israel is due to the policy regarding Arabs, with so much indifference that is reflected in the reduction of their rights through discrimination that exert Israeli civilian and military authorities against the Palestinians. Even Israel has built exclusive roads for Jews who live in settlements in the occupied territories of the West Bank. The rights of the Palestinians have been reduced so much that the Gaza Strip resembles a giant jail without roof. So, Carter exposes analogously, establishing a correlation of the treatment given to the Palestinians under the occupation force, with the treatments that in its moment, had received the black people when they were subordinated to the system of Apartheid in South Africa, which in Spanish is known as racial segregation.

Most of authorities in Israel, have shocked with rage whenever they hear the term apartheid, when Carter refers to the Israeli-Palestinian conflict, especially because it comes from a book written by a famous politician who showed special sympathy toward Israel during his mandate but the exploration with honesty and justice, ended up tipping the balance towards the side that Israel dislikes; the truth.

On the other hand, former President Carter had the courage to present his work in a nation such as the United States where the manipulation of the media on Palestine topic, had had under deception over many years to many American citizens. Therefore, with this criterion, carter intends to show the reality of the events in the occupied territories, though it falls pretty badly in the Jewish lobby, which they see how its castle of lies and deception begins to collapse.

At the beginning of the year 2012, the renowned professor of the Hebrew University of Jerusalem Nurit Peled Elhanan, published a book where, basically, was denouncing the radical school program that the authorities of Israel provide to Israeli children at their schools. The title of the book "Palestine in school textbooks: ideology and propaganda in education". In this work, the Israeli author reveals the systematic operation of brain washing and manipulation exerted on the small Jewish children in order to create rejection and hatred against Arabs and particularly the Palestinians that ends up convincing them that they are enemies to eliminate. Thus this teacher became a researcher at first hand to analyze textbooks that Israeli children receive. She came to the conclusion that the psychological effect is overwhelming, so they see the Palestinians as a backward society, where the Israeli children should not have sensitive towards them; can you imagine those Israeli children converted in soldiers? Obviously the Zionist organizations were "creative" to develop these school primers.

This citizen and Israeli academic, expert in literature and education, has been denouncing the racist profile that the authorities of Israel have given to education, focused primarily to discredit the Palestinians, presenting them as enemies of Israel. She had to live her own hard experience with the bitter taste of the conflict when lost a young daughter in a suicide bombing carried out by a Palestinian, but always remained in her position in the sense of demonstrating total disagreement with the Israeli policy of occupation, as her vertical rejection towards the policy of construction of Jewish settlements in the occupied territories. She does not hesitate to blame Israel for the death of her daughter due to the hatred and resentment that they have originated in the Palestinian population, as result of the unjust and racist policies against the Palestinians and in addition to that, the constant confiscation of land, in order to build more settlements for new Jewish immigrants. For having the courage to speak in favor of the Palestinian cause and against the policy of Israeli occupation, in 2001 the European Parliament recognized her effort for peace and for that reason, was awarded with the Sakharov Prize.

The intuition of this woman is admirable since she examined the hostile behavior of Israeli soldiers against Palestinians and after a serious investigative exploration, came to the conclusion that the problem originates in the educational system of Israel. When an Israeli citizen completes high school and is at the doors of becoming an adult, is ready for the army with a definite image of what the Palestinians are, because they are seen with a sign that says "terrorists". Those young soldiers lose the human sensibility towards the Palestinian people.

By Kassem Asmar Castellanos

Nurit Peled, denounces the Israeli blatant manipulation of the history and the contemporary facts that have direct relation with the Palestinian people, since the Zionists never write about the demographic and geographic statistics of the Palestinian people and much less when it comes to illustrate maps in Israeli school textbooks, as if the Palestinian people had never inhabited these lands. When they show many Jewish settlements in the West Bank, are illustrated in particular way, as if Palestinians don't live around those illegal settlements. The idea is to try to justify the presence of those Jewish settlers in the occupied territories. They always show how primitive are the Palestinians and without progress. About the expulsion of Palestinians, even in the period that preceded the creation of the State of Israel, those school primers deny that there have been such expulsions, moreover the Zionists deny that the Palestinians have been abused, simply that those who left, did so on a voluntary way. In Israel, most time the Palestinians are mentioned as Arabs with the aim to convince the Israeli citizens that the Palestinians have where to go, since there are many Arab countries. For that reason, Israel calls them as Palestinian, when they are related to the term "terrorist".

Anyway, Nurit Peled never tires to defend Palestinians' human rights and holds firmly the conviction that the policy that Israel intends to keep with the occupation of the West Bank, next to the Jewish settlements, it has become a contention wall against any attempt of peace in the region.

By Kassem Asmar Castellanos

5. THE SEPARATION WALL; A STRATEGY THAT GOES BEYOND THE ISSUE OF SECURITY

In 2002, Prime Minister Ariel Sharon found a green light for a project that had been approved by his government. This project consisted of raising different kinds of walls and electrified fences in order to prevent the entry of Palestinian terrorists and avoid suicide attacks against Israeli inhabitants. Well, that was apparently, the reason for the construction of that wall which it had to meander throughout the occupied territories, although while the construction was advancing, the evidences and purposes showed that the real objective of this wall, was going far beyond the issue of security.

In order to have an idea of the tremendous trip that Israel did to the Palestinians and the international community with this illegal construction, let us start from the fact that the green line, is the border demarcation which the law and international juridical system had established in 1949 to separate Israel from West Bank, it has a length of approximately 360 km and if we take into account that the wall and electrified fences that separate the West Bank from Israel it has a path of 720 km, i.e. it measures twice the length of the green line border. We realize without having to resort to complex research centers that Israel committed an assault, regardless of the international legal order, confiscating more Palestinian territories of the West Bank, which amount to 9% of the West Bank.

Clear evidence that their argument plague of deception and lies is in the fact that Israel has as a pretext for the construction of the wall, the Palestinian suicide operations on Israeli territory, and the questions that millions of people do in different places of the world, are the followings; for ensuring the Israeli safety, should they steal and confiscate Palestinian territories of the West Bank, getting beyond the green line border? Should they steal dozens of water wells, destroying homes and causing displacements? For the Israeli security, must they destroy the cultivated land of many Palestinians and give it to Jewish settlers of the settlements?

By Kassem Asmar Castellanos

A few months later that the Zionist regime had begun the construction of the wall, Israel didn't respect a Resolution of UN's assembly in 2003, which demanded the immediate cessation of such construction, added to a clear decision in 2004 by the ICJ (International Court of Justice) in the sense that the wall in itself it is a flagrant violation of human rights and international humanitarian law, also lacks all ethical and moral coherence, since it was found that the purpose of the wall and the fact that the layout of the same does not respect at all the green line border, it can be concluded that the objectives of the wall, holds other interests for the State of Israel.

Moreover, Amnesty International had already issued a statement through which considered that the wall has no justification and that it clearly violates international legal principle, when Israel takes possession of fact, part of the occupied territories of the West Bank with the abusive route of the wall to "protect" its illegal colonists who live in settlements in the West Bank. Statistics show that there are more than 530,000 Jewish colonists in West Bank soil, living in the middle of 2.5 million Palestinians.

It is estimated that 82% of the wall route, enters into the occupied territories. To raise the wall, many Palestinian houses were demolished and all cultivation that the arbitrary path found in its way was also destroyed. Additional lands were confiscated and many inhabitants belonging to more than 40 villages, were isolated between the wall and the green line and more of the third part, were completely surrounded and enclosed by the wall, as ghetto style.

To protect approximately 50 Jewish settlements, Israel designed the route of the wall as an excuse to justify once more, the spiral of violations of the Palestinian sovereignty to seize an important part of the West Bank. In a way, we are talking about 9% of the West Bank, which in itself is very small since it does not exceed 5,600 Km^2.

The wall has meant for many Palestinians a padlock around their necks, because has fragmented Arab populations in something like ghettos or cantons. In fact, more than 240 Km^2 of cultivable lands and about 50 wells in the West Bank ended up in the hands of Israel and its settlers, all this due to the racist route of the wall.

91

By Kassem Asmar Castellanos

Photo 4. Source AFP. "The separation wall built by Israel"

The Palestinians were restricted to live in a permanent division of their territory. Those Palestinians who left between the wall and the green line, their quality of life got worse. This situation affects more than 40 Palestinian villages.

There are many checkpoints along the wall and the problem for many Palestinians is that to go to the other side, there is no other way but through them. For example, if a Palestinian wants to go to his working place which is a few kilometers away from his home, must do a long tour since he has to reach those sites of entry and exit that were put in different sections of the wall and must take in mind that these sites have opening and closing times. Numerous Palestinians have to wait for a long time, until the Zionist soldiers open the gates to get access, which becomes a humiliation for many Palestinians. However, those kinds of obstacles or difficulties are not specific for workers; students of all levels have to deal with those obstacles imposed by the occupying forces. The wall also entails obstacles for any diligence or service that many of the Palestinians want to get access. For example, if someone wants to do any job or personal procedure, must take into account the time that will spend the route, from home to the place where he wants to go.

Statistical data show that because of the wall, many Palestinians have lost their jobs for being repeatedly late, to the places of work. Palestinian farmers have felt the rigors and abuse that the wall has meant for them, because many cases of Palestinians whose livelihoods are derived from agricultural activity but, because of their lands stayed on the other side of the wall and the difficulties of getting there are hard and if we add the restricted schedule imposed by the Zionist military authorities, inevitably all these measures have been causing the loss of many crops that end up forcing the Palestinian farmers, to abandon their main activity.

Another obstacle that appears for farmers, is when they want to sell their products in different parts of the West Bank since the route that they should do, can become in headache and humiliation, accompanied with a feeling of impotence especially because are perishable products. Isn't this what Israel always wanted in the sense to force the Palestinian farmers to leave their lands and in this way, to be exploited by Jewish settlers who live in the settlements?

In addition, every Palestinian must carry a special permit according to the place where he wants to go. For example, he has to clarify if is going to work, or to a health post, a school, somewhere in agricultural work, etc. The fact that they have to wait until they can pass the checkpoints, make feel to the Palestinians like prisoners, within their territory and with a trend of frustration. In the case of Jerusalem city, Israel has radicalized its position against the Palestinians since the Zionist state declared Jerusalem as its indivisible capital.

After the 1967 war, Israel expelled many Palestinians and confiscated large tracts of land in order to build enough settlements. The siege of eastern Jerusalem which belongs to Palestinians, it shows how the Zionists disobeyed international laws. On this point, the UN Security Council spoke out through Resolution 478, which declared illegal and unacceptable Israeli measure. Israel has implemented a strict policy of Judaizing Jerusalem.

By Kassem Asmar Castellanos

Since long ago, the Palestinians of the West Bank (the eastern part of Jerusalem is a part of the West Bank) cannot visit freely any place of Jerusalem, unless they have a special permit that would justify this visit. Access for reaching the Holy City is through the famous checkpoints, which surround the city of Jerusalem. If some sick Palestinian wants to get to a hospital in Jerusalem, he must be transferred in another ambulance that has Israeli number plates, but the patient must have a permit to go into Jerusalem, regardless of his state of health. The situation became more difficult because the route of the wall, has made that a large extent of East Jerusalem remains on the Israeli side and many Palestinians were isolated from the West Bank since the wall surrounds them, and so many other reasons that has turned life of the Palestinians in a picture of more humiliation, with the complicity of the international community that doesn't go beyond a simple and theoretical conviction. If quality of life under Israeli occupation was difficult, it has become even more complex as a result of the lifting of the wall.

One of the rules that most protect the international law is the freedom of movement, which says that any citizen within its territory can choose his place of residence and the ease of mobility. Amnesty International has said several times that the break of the norms of international law committed by Israel with the consequences for daily life of the Palestinians with the lifting of the wall is very evident. Moreover, the confiscation of lands to the Palestinians with the intention to pass them to the hands of the Jewish colonists who are "protected" by the wall is simply a terrestrial piracy of an outsized outrage and abuse by the Zionist military authorities, carried out with the blessing of the central Israeli government and obviously with the plausible posture that keeps the U.S. Government.

The insolence and the cynicism of the Israeli Government exceed, completely, the limits of shamelessness, when says that Israel has the right to annex part of the West Bank territory for "security reasons" and so, is "necessary" the destruction of Palestinian homes, the confiscation and theft of lands and the destruction of agricultural fields.

By Kassem Asmar Castellanos

When the issue was debated at the end of 2003 in the ICJ (International Court of Justice), the sentence against the construction of the wall was overwhelming since 15 judges that make up that Court, 14 voted against Israel to demand them to stop every kind of work related to the construction of the wall, because this violates flagrantly, the international law. Also, demanded that Israel dismantles the built sections. The only vote that didn't want to join to the unanimous ruling was the United States, although it was not difficult to anticipate. Hours later, Israel through its brilliant Prime Minister Ariel Sharon, said that the ruling of the ICJ will go into the dustbin of history.

Israel is the state that more times has trampled and violated Resolutions and opinions of the international community and indeed has done it for 65 years, so it is not surprising its position, which is bolstered by American support. In the current conditions, it is not possible to build a real independent Palestinian State, because under the Israeli racist policies, the West Bank stayed fragmented into several pieces. To cite a few examples: on one hand we have Qalqilya, Jenin and Salfit, on the other hand Bethlehem and Hebron. So it is not astonishing that Israel is perceived as a state that applies discriminatory policies and Apartheid. Why is it a state with Apartheid and racist system?, because it is illegal the confiscating of Palestinian lands, also, because destroys homes, limits access to work and to freedom of movement to the Palestinian people, isolates many peasants and farmers from their agricultural lands and applies discriminatory rules that favor Jewish settlers in the West Bank.

It is clear that the wall built by Israel, in fact way, has taken over of 9% of the West Bank, but it should not be forgotten that the Zionist plan of Theodor Herzel, devised in the Jewish Congress in Basel in the late 19th century and ratified in the ideology of the Zionist leader Ben Gurion, when he hinted that the true intentions of Zionism and Jewish leaders was to take control of the whole Palestine. The Zionist snare in Palestine has been like a cancer that has spread slowly to every corner of the Palestinian territories in order to populate them with Jewish immigrants, and at the same time, expel their rightful owners who are Palestinians that have lived those lands, throughout centuries.

By Kassem Asmar Castellanos

The outlook at present is as follows; there is a hostile occupying force called Israel, and a population who wants to get rid of the yoke that represents the Zionist occupation forces. The things must be called by its name and the invading State is Israel that insists on ignoring many decisions and Resolutions that demand the Zionists to put once and for all, an end to its policy of occupation of the Palestinian territories. That pretext of Israel's security is fairly shortsighted, by reason of that the true security lies in recognizing the right of the Palestinian people to self-determination and that is achieved when Israel takes the commitment and the determination to withdraw its military troops from the occupied territories and removes all its illegal Jewish settlements.

Currently, Israel has more than 78% of what was Palestine until 1947, i.e. Before the Declaration of independence of Israel at the United Nations in 1948 because of the disgraceful assault that the Zionism made in the main precinct of the UN, with the complicity of several countries led by the United States in order to ensure any way, the needed votes for the creation of Israel, therefore, the cynicism of Israel has no precedent in history, due to that the Zionists has stolen more than $\frac{3}{4}$ parts of Palestine, however have the insolence to not withdraw from what little is left of the Palestinian first territory.

By Kassem Asmar Castellanos

6. THE GAZA STRIP, LIVING WITH THE SIEGE AND THE ISRAELI BLOCKADE

The Gaza Strip it is a territory with a rectangular appearance of about 360 Km2, part of that territory is arid, but another part is suitable for farming. It is along a coastline of 40 Km whose shores are bathed by the Mediterranean Sea. One of the things that catch the eye is that Gaza is one of the most densely populated regions in the world with 1,500,000 inhabitants. This gives us a record of 4,160 inhabitants per Km2. To understand what we are talking about, we have the following didactic example; imagine La Gomera, which is a beautiful island of Spain, with 1,500,000 inhabitants, (Gomera island has no more than 25,000 inhabitants).

Unfortunately, in the last years, sad stories and hostile situations have been linked to Gaza in the news of the different media around the world that has had this kind of headlines from the Gaza Strip. Nonetheless, the difficulties of its people started in early 1948 and before the creation of the State of Israel. Due to the fact that being a region of high demographic concentration, has its explanation in the exodus of Al Nakba when many of these exiles, went to the Gaza Strip, especially after the first Arab-Israeli war of 1948.

The refugees in the Gaza Strip have had the status of Palestinian refugees by Egyptian authorities after 1950 when this country came to be the administrator of that small Palestinian territory. Although part of the population of Gaza has always lived there since a long time, a chain of Palestinian refugees began to arrive because of the mass expulsion that suffered, after 1948 in the sadly famous Al Nakba. Therefore, this fraction of Palestine took place under supervision of Egypt and the only document that its inhabitants could carry, was one whose distinction clearly said "Palestinian refugee". This measure was imposed for all residents of Gaza, why? The answer is easy. Egypt neither should, nor could morally grant Palestinians the Egyptian nationality because it could automatically translate as a support to the Israeli strategy of separating by any means possible, Palestine from the Palestinians. So, the historical responsibility of the Israeli authorities to populate the Palestinian territories with Jews settlers, under no circumstances could have the blessing of the Egyptian authorities by action or omission.

Basically, this was the reason for not granting the Egyptian citizenship to many Palestinians. Anyway, the other Arab countries that welcomed the Palestinian refugees, not only from 1948 but also those who came after the 1967 war, also, assumed this same decision. The inhabitants of the Gaza Strip, while they were under the administration of Egypt, it did not indicate that they had the right to enter this territory and establish their residences in the heart of Egypt, due to the above reason and the commitment of Egypt with the Palestinians it was limited to that strip. Very few inhabitants of Gaza had received temporary Jordanian passports in order to travel through airports.

After 1967 and once that Arab-Israeli war had finished, the demographic situation in Gaza had grown with the arriving of other refugees and the dynamics of its population growth. Zionist occupation authorities gave all the inhabitants of the Gaza Strip, an Israeli identity card. Additionally to this document, there is another that should be used whenever the people of Gaza want to leave that part of Palestine. What did happen with the inhabitants of Gaza who went to live elsewhere before the 1967 war? They stayed definitely without homeland, same as the exiles of 1948. In other words, they stayed without territorial identity and the main Israeli pretext was that those Palestinians that were not registered in the Israeli list after the 1967 war, did not have the right to return and much less to residence. Only those who later proved that had direct families of first grade consanguinity established in Gaza, could get a special permit to visit them. Described in another way, many Palestinians in Gaza returned as very temporary visitors and that would be equivalent to say that they were simple tourists. The Palestinians, like simple temporary visitors within its territory! If this in itself is a humiliation, is not less humiliating that when a Gaza's inhabitant decides to travel should ask permission to the authorities of Israel, with the aim to get a very temporary special document which highlights the terms "nationality undetermined or undefined". But the absence is subject to what is indicated in that document, if an one-year permit was obtained, it should return to Gaza before the year expires, otherwise, this Palestinian citizen can lose his right in Gaza. All this has a very blunt explanation since the Zionist authorities have applied dissuasive and abusive tactics, with the basic goal of shrink up the standard and condition of living of the inhabitants of Gaza and with this outlook, many people feel forced to go out to seek their livelihood in other countries. Obviously, the visible and brazen tactics of the Zionist authorities lie in the fact that set a specific date, for the return of those who decided to leave due to perfectly understandable reasons, whose main motive is to seek the livelihood for their families and this should not be determined for short periods as were established by the authorities of Israel who end up "justifying" the prohibition of return to those who did not "respect" the date limit that the authorities of Israel had established.

But if these treatments were classified as unfair and racist, making difficult the conditions of many inhabitants of Gaza which became more difficult after the Gulf war following the Iraqi invasion to Kuwait and the unexpected backing of the leader of the PLO (Palestine Liberation Organization) Yasser Arafat to Saddam Hussein which resulted, after the war, in the expulsion of thousands of Palestinians mainly from Kuwait, and to a lesser quantity from Iraq and elsewhere in the Gulf. It was estimated that 300,000 Palestinians approximately, were expelled. Some of them belonged to the Gaza Strip but they were established in Kuwait by job issues, but had to face this sad reality, since they could not return to Gaza for the simple reason that the Israeli authorities impeded it, because they were not considered citizens of the Gaza Strip. Then, what did happen? This people had to choose to establish their residences in other Arab countries with the benevolence of their governments.

The hard truth raised by Zionist leaders is that Gaza inhabitants, who were living outside, had no right in Palestine, particularly in Gaza. Although the social and economic situation imposed on the residents of Gaza, it wasn't something inherent only to this strip, since the Zionist occupation authorities after 1967 did the same thing in the West Bank and all those who were not registered in the census that did the authorities of Israel, therefore considered Palestinians without right of residence and without possibility of returning permanently. How is that understood? Basically are admitted as 3rd class tourists with a defined time. The Israeli authorities had compressed to the maximum the right

By Kassem Asmar Castellanos

of the Palestinian people, with the legendary Palestine, cutting the historical ties, which for centuries had established the Palestinians in this region. Anyway wasn't this, the strategy of the Zionist movements that were backed by the military and economic support of the British, French and Americans? It's clear that the different procedures of the Israeli authorities, in relation to the systematic reduction of the presence of Palestinians after 1948, had become a state policy that was seen by their supporters and followers of the West as a plausible measure.

Then, how do the authorities of Israel distinguish that a Palestinian belongs to a restricted region of the occupied territories? By the color of their documents that every Palestinian citizen has and the Israeli military authorities in any checkpoint decide how far they can go, even if a Palestinian citizen is looking for a job. This makes that the Zionist authorities restrict the movements of the Palestinians inside the occupied territories and especially if somebody intends to look for a job in the territories of Israel, i.e. which was established in 1948. This scene shows the discriminatory treatment they receive in Palestine and much more within Israel, since the Palestinians receive a salary lower in comparison with the wages that Israelis receive.

After several meetings between Israeli and Palestinian representatives and after having signed the Oslo accords, Israel withdrew from the territory of Gaza though Hammas does not recognize the agreements reached in Oslo. By the way, it is right to clarify that the dismantling of settlements in Gaza where were living, Jewish colonists until 2005, basically, was given by the lack of interest of the State of Israel of maintaining less than 9,000 settlers Jews near almost 1,500,000 Palestinians from Gaza, and on this topic in a previous section in this same book was explained.

Today, almost 70% of Gaza's population lives in poverty, so Gaza depends on external aid. Although the Jewish settlements were dismantled, Gaza is surrounded by Israeli military points along the 50 Km of border that has with Israel. Especially since Hammas took power in 2006, when the situation became very sensitive as a result of the determination of the leaders of Hammas militias for launching their handmade rockets to Israel but, this situation has been exploited by Israel to respond with excessive military reaction against the region, causing great destruction, reflected in human lives and infrastructure. In addition, Israel continued pressuring the Palestinian residents of Gaza by limiting, in exaggerated extent, transit of goods and other humanitarian aids.

Another fact that made Israel radicalize its position, affecting the inhabitants of Gaza was the Palestinian popular uprising against occupation and Israeli discriminatory measures against the Palestinians in the year 2000, worldwide known as the Intifada and who put the image of Israel in bad position in the eyes of the international public opinion. The international aid to Gaza has been limited since many countries of the International community don't recognize Hammas as the representative of the Palestinian people, also most of the Western countries are reluctant to accept Hammas as the legitimate representative of the Palestinians because they consider it a terrorist movement. That has made that Israel applies a policy against their inhabitants, cutting off many times the provision of basic things as food, fuel and medicines, arguing that those shipments may contain weapons for Hammas, but on the other hand, preventing the Palestinians take out their agricultural products from Gaza.

In early 2008, several international organizations of NGOs (non-governmental organization) had come to the conclusion that the Palestinians in the Gaza Strip were living the worst situation of the past 40 years, qualifying that territory as a large prison in the free air. Much of that guilt must be assumed by the same State of Israel for its exaggerated blockade to the Strip that restricts the mobility of its inhabitants. This practice resulted in an increase in unemployment of more than 38%. Economically, Gaza remains static in the limbo of backwardness because projects are not easy to carry out with the permanent Israeli military blockade. With constant cuts that Israel makes in the supply of electric power, life in Gaza is simply hopeless; additionally we must add the bad quality of water that the people consume.

The international community strongly opposes the application of exaggerated and collective punishment imposed by Israel to all residents of Gaza. In practical terms, the current situation of their inhabitants is worse than days under Israeli occupation. This paradoxical situation is due to that Israel does what it wants;

By Kassem Asmar Castellanos

breaking the principles of international law, which condemns any kind of hostility and collective punishment against the defenseless people of Gaza. If that was not enough, the Zionist state has an almost absolute control to the use of the airspace, maritime and land in Gaza and its surroundings. So in practice, it continues being a symbolic event for the inhabitants of Gaza " withdrawal of Israel" from the Gaza Strip under the Oslo agreement.

Even in 2007 the Secretary General of the UN Ban Ki-moon told that with such hostile policies, Israel violates the principles of international humanitarian law, attempting without distinction against the civilian population of Gaza. This inhumane Israeli practice has collapsed the economy of the region so much that the poverty is clear in many places in Gaza where the degree of vulnerability, requires them to be on the threshold of survival with the help coming from different international sources. The lack of respect and obeisance by Israel to minimum standards of civilization and its contempt, towards the human right statutes, established by the international legality, is reflected in its criminal behavior such as that carried out in mid- 2010 against a ship that carried humanitarian aid for Gaza, known as the "fleet of freedom" whose operation had the support of several NGOs. These boats with food supplies, suffered a military assault of maritime piracy that ended with the death of nine Turkish pacifists. The cynicism of Israel reached such point that it forced the Government of Turkey to break all diplomatic ties with Israel since not only Israel refused to offer apologies to the Government of Ankara, but also the Zionist Government accused the murdered Turkish activists of belonging to terrorist networks. The calm waters of the Mediterranean Sea were silent witnesses of that collective murder.

In March 2013, U.S. President Barak Obama on a visit to Israel and showing his usual role as ally of the Zionist State, wanted to offer a good detail in favor of his Zionist friends, mediating in the restoration of the diplomatic relations between Israel and Turkey. Obviously, the effort was not so difficult, except several phone calls accompanied by a few bilateral smiles.

By Kassem Asmar Castellanos

In January 2008 the inhabitants of Gaza reached such degree of hardship and despair to get some basic products to appease the needs of most vulnerable population of Gaza such as children and the elderly and avoid them from collapsing due to the lack of food, forced a group of young men in Gaza to break several sections of the border of Rafah which separates them from Egypt with the intention of acquiring the most elementary things needed for their population. Egypt could not prevent that fact because it was a humanitarian reaction. Obviously, this scenery so cruel and inhuman that has exposed the Hebrew State, turning it into an excuse to promote its Zionist plans, to continue activating their strategies of many years ago, even before the creation of the State of Israel that consists of changing at any cost, the geographical outlook in the region of Palestine. This is because in recent years, Israel has felt increasing concern towards the Palestinian population, because does not stop its demographic increase that has undergone since 20 years. We can conclude that this suffocating padlock to Gaza and West Bank has response to this Machiavellian Zionist vision of undermining the will of the Palestinian people and force them to emigrate out of Palestine and pretend to present them as voluntary emigrants. This is the perspective that Israel wants to design for showing that Jews are the deserving of those Palestinian lands by simple arithmetic question which is that they are a majority.

Argentinian journalist Hernan Zin could narrate with great detail in a work known as "Rains on Gaza", the horrors that without distinction lived its inhabitants and ensures that what he saw in Afghanistan, Somalia, Sudan, Congo and elsewhere, is less delicate according what he had to see, in Gaza. This author explains the dramatic and cruel results of the Israeli military operation that launched against the Gaza Strip in mid-2006 known as "summer rain". Hernan Zin narrates that Israeli Government's determination of attacking Gaza through this operation, came after the Palestinian popular militia killed two Israeli soldiers and a third fell captive and subsequently retained, that soldier was the Corporal Gilad Salid. The Argentinian journalist was appalled to see the degree of blockade and siege that the people of Gaza had endured, where all kinds of food supply were cut. Israel also attacked electrical installations and prohibited that patients could be treated in hospitals outside Gaza, preventing the departure of patients and ambulances. Continues Hernan Zin recounting in his book that the quality of life of the Palestinian residents of Gaza is on the edge of misery when at the same time, Israeli citizens who are meters from Gaza, live a life of comfort and without any kind of needs. The narration of this Argentinian journalist is an objective testimony, as a result of direct experiences that had felt in the place of the events and deserve total credibility.

Photo 5. Source REUTERS. "Funeral of Turkish activists in Istanbul, killed by Israel as they were heading to Gaza with an aid boat"

Anyway, the Israeli operation "summer rain" reflects the racist spirit of Zionism and the State of Israel. If by the death of two soldiers and the abduction of a third, Israel decided to attack savagely Gaza, also submit the Palestinian population of more than 1,500,000 inhabitants, under a cruel siege and blockade, accompanied by infernal bombings with more than 450 people dead, most of them defenseless civilians and additionally to cause enormous damage to many infrastructures and housing. If this is

By Kassem Asmar Castellanos

not conclusive proof of a criminal racism, then what name does it deserve? We shouldn't forget that punishment and collective hostilities violate the most basic rules of the Geneva Conventions.

Moreover, the Israeli argument that tries to justify the endless blockade and military response that imposes on Gaza, in response to the throwing of the Qassam rockets by militias of Hammas, is grossly disproportionate and deadly and that jumps to the view with the amount of death and destruction by the Palestinian side.

In November 2012, using the same argument, Israel launched a disproportionate operation called 'defensive pillar' and similar to the previous military operations, it left great devastation on the Palestinian side. Israel justified its action saying that it was to stop the terrorist activities of Hammas.

The obligatory question arises, when Israel applies its racist and discriminatory State policy to destroy with its huge excavators and tractors, crop, water storage wells and the siege to Gaza fishermen, even shooting so that they do not pass the five miles from their shores, abusive measure imposed by Israel and this has happened too often in recent years. These hostile practices against the inhabitants of Gaza, that is a racist State policy, approved and applauded by the Zionist right-wing politicians, are not clear evidence of State terrorism? Many countries have condemned these criminal practices and the only country turns a blind eye is the United States, eternal mentor and ally who allows Israel to do everything, in the name of the worn out phrase: "the right to legitimate defense". Ultimately, the United States considers Israel its huge military base in this important geopolitical region of the Middle East, and when manages the Israeli-Palestinian issue, the U.S speech that is used elsewhere in the world in terms of freedom and justice, goes to the background.

Fishing is a very important line of the economy but fishers only use small boats which turns this activity very limited, moreover, they cannot fish beyond ten kilometers away of the Gaza Strip, although when Israel decides to make restrictions, the fishers can only reach five kilometers from the coast. However, it is a central line of the limited economy of the region and added to agriculture activity, allows partly mitigate the enormous needs of Gaza. But the main obstacle continues being the abusive measures of Israel, which limits the trade of many products from Gaza to avoid that they become competitive with products of Israeli agricultural crops. This Zionist tactic has forced many farmers in the Gaza Strip to desist from cultivating their lands and has ended up as employees on the other side, working in Israeli agriculture.

All these practices of Israel impede the growth of the economy in the West Bank and the Gaza Strip, limiting their opportunities that barely reaches the threshold for the survival of its inhabitants. Whenever there is a siege and Israeli blockade on Gaza, it means a strangulation of its economy because much of the clothing manufactured in Gaza, is for the West Bank and Israeli markets. The situation is worse with many agricultural products were part of them is destined for the European market. On the three occasions that Israel ruthlessly attacked Gaza, whose operations were named as "summer rain", "cast lead" and "defensive pillar', also the hostile punishment to many Palestinians for having participated in the popular uprisings against the Israeli occupation and its racist policies and discrimination, world-famous as the Intifadas, has left the economy of the Gaza Strip at the edge of the abyss and only the tenacity and spirit of endurance of its inhabitants It has allowed them not to collapse entirely.

Water is very scarce in Gaza, since it can't to arrive because Israel collects it in the course of its route of the subsoil of Negev to their citizens. It is humiliating that having lots of water that comes from the occupied territories, Gaza's inhabitants have to pay high tariff, and if we add the electricity cuts that Israel carries out often, this translates into an ordeal for farmers because they cannot irrigate their crops with the periodicity required, therefore many products are damaged. Obviously, because of this situation, many farmers opt to leave this work. On the other hand, others prefer to continue with farming but with some obligatory changes, using another kind of crops that need less water but generate less profit. In this case, stop to grow some vegetables and fruits to replace them with wheat. At the end and after all, that's what Israel wants that nobody can compete with its products. Agriculture sector is not only important for farmers, but also is very important for its own population. In addition it is a source of generation of

106

employments; especially if we take into account that today, Gaza has one of the highest unemployment rates in the world of about 38%. Agricultural supplies are usually achieved with very high prices by the permanent blockade due to the Israeli authorities. Fishing has become a hard activity since the Palestinians cannot get into the water beyond ten kilometers in normal times or five kilometers from the coast when there are siege and blockade. This makes fishing activity be very limited and poor so it is estimated that more than half of the fishermen have left that job. This kind of practice, which is part of the discriminatory policy of the State of Israel against the Palestinians, violates an agreement in Oslo, which stipulates that Gaza Strip fishermen can fish 20 nautical miles from its coast, but Israel has record in violation of the most elementary rules of international law. In fact, its contempt for not respecting the international legality, date from 1948 until the present day. We must not forget that in 1948, Israel began to show his scorn toward the legal principles, established by the international community when it rejected the implementation of the Resolution 194, decreed by the General Assembly of the United Nations that demanded Israel, to allow those Palestinians who were forced to leave their homes and Lands, the right to return and those which for several reasons did not want to return to the newly created Jewish State, should have given them financial compensation.

You don't have to feel surprised when Israel derides of the most elementary rules of legitimacy of the civilized international community because that makes part of its racist views and foreign policy. The brazenness of the authorities of Israel comes to such an extent that says what type of products should be produced by the people of the Gaza Strip and which can be exported in limited quantities, i.e., the allowed quantities. They do this to promote agricultural activity in Israel and obviously favoring the Israeli farmers.

It is estimated that since 2007 until the present date, the incomes from agricultural activity have declined 40%, coinciding with the siege and the exaggerated Israeli blockade. The barriers that Israel has imposed on exports of agricultural products from Gaza to the West Bank, Israel and Europe, has forced many families to set aside this important labor for their economy. This has made

By Kassem Asmar Castellanos

that the statistic on unemployment has increased, although other items of their economy, have also suffered from this crisis.

If we take into account that to all of the above, it must be added the fact that Palestinians in Gaza, most of them, can't go to work in the West Bank because under the rules of the Zionist occupation forces, they are considered illegal and this kind of actions continues being unbelievable by the cynicism and racism due to the meaning of those measures. It sounds absurd that a Palestinian from Gaza cannot move with some freedom in the occupied Palestinian territories but that is the reality. Obviously there has not been even a remote possibility that an inhabitant of Gaza, tries to get permanent residence in West Bank.

Anyway, the tenacity, the faith and an unbreakable spirit of this ancient people of Gaza and their optimism to a more just future, allows them to reach the following conclusion: it is worthwhile to continue living under the glow of the sky despite the dark blockade and Israeli siege.

By *Kassem Asmar Castellanos*

7. THE PALESTINIANS IN NABLUS, HEBRON, BETHLEHEM, QALQILYA, JENIN AND JERUSALEM, UNDER THE OCCUPATION FORCES

The purpose of this chapter is to continue exposing the difficult conditions of the Palestinian people in the occupied territories, especially from 1967 when all Palestine was surrounded by the tentacles of Zionism which did not save efforts, nor imagination to complete of implementing the expansionist and racist ideology inherent in Zionist thinking that has caused a huge damage against the Palestinians. In this sense, we have to be clear by saying that this control which the occupation authority have been exerting to avoid that it comes to the light of the international community, news and information from different parts of the West Bank, has been hard. Obviously, the objective is that the world does not know what is happening with the Palestinians that live under the Israeli occupation and besides, prevent complaints to transcend to important media. Therefore, the next exposition is a clear reflection of the daily life of the Palestinians in these occupied territories and dominated by the racist rules of the Zionist state.

Nablus is a city that has around 140,000 inhabitants although if we count the municipalities and Palestinian villages that are in the periphery, which belong to the region of Nablus, add up 360,000 inhabitants approximately. This city is to the North of the occupied territories by Israel, and the name comes from the Roman era. One can say that Nablus is one of the oldest cities in the world although it is divided in two; which constituted the Romans and later which was founded by the Ottomans (today Turkey). Up until the year 2000, there was some economic stability in the city (if this term fits under the Israeli occupation forces) but as a result of the second Intifada or Palestinian resistance against the Israeli occupation and discrimination policies, Israel imposed severe punishment not only from the economic view point, but also many Palestinian protesters were killed in the streets of Nablus. Many historical and modern buildings were damaged by Israeli military incursions, i.e., an important part of the Palestinian cultural heritage was significantly damaged, in violation of an international

By Kassem Asmar Castellanos

agreement that protects cultural property when there is a conflict. This right was established by the Hague Convention and the IV Geneva Convention, signed by many countries including Israel. But, is Israel worried about this international legal norm?

This city has the virtue that coexist together, Christians and Palestinian Muslims without drawbacks. Here were destroyed ancient places such as the Museum that is a very old factory of soaps, Turkish baths, among others. Obviously these attacks affect the city's historic weight.

Every day, the Israeli soldiers patrol the streets of Nablus with total freedom, especially at night and that makes Palestinians feel wrapped in a kind of uncertainty and if that was not enough, Jewish colonists from the closer settlements to the city make mischief under the Israeli soldiers' protection. For example, Jewish colonists from three settlements that are Brecham, Yitzhar and Shilo, arrived in a rural area next to Nablus and burned crops especially the ancient crops, that are olive trees and attacked Palestinian farmers. The seriousness of this fact is that Israeli soldiers were accomplices by omission because didn't prevent these hostile actions against Palestinians in Nablus. A young Palestinian died in this incident.

It is important to clarify that Israel, rarely punishes a Jewish citizen if kills a Palestinian since they can plead self-defense but the case is that the racist system does what is necessary to exempt, from any punishment to any Israeli citizen, with a snap of total impunity. It is common to see Jewish colonists throwing stones at Palestinian children who go on school buses. The situation get worse after the Intifadas since it could perceive in the impoverished life of its inhabitants, and in the level of unemployment. Like most of the occupied territories, Nablus has an economy that just allows its villagers to survive. On the other hand, its economic activities are based on Agriculture (with all the difficulties involved this activity, because of is very difficult to get water for these tasks), soap production, olive oil and some crafts are activities of most of Nablus' inhabitants, but the rest of the population that are many, is part of the statistic of those who are unemployed.

By Kassem Asmar Castellanos

There are several refugee camps that are home to about 60,000 Palestinians, on the same edge of Nablus and date back to the time of the Al Nakba when they were forced to leave their lands and homes that were later given to the immigrant Jews, after the 1948 Israeli-Arab war. If there is a part of Palestine whose people has gone against the Israeli occupation in an explicit and consistent way, are the inhabitants of Nablus. Indeed, part of their everyday lives is to see in many places and corners of Nablus, large posters with the faces of those who have lost their lives in defense of the emancipation and against Israeli occupation. Deservedly, they are declared martyrs of the Palestinian cause.

It is not easy to get to Nablus by the number of checkpoints that must be passed to reach the city. The paradox is despite the fact this city offers many attractions that date from several centuries ago, the city is not touristic. Obviously, the Government of Israel, as it has happened with other parts of the Palestinian territories, doesn't want cities like Nablus have much contact with the outside through tourism, with the aim of hiding the truth that lies behind the Israeli occupation. It is very clear that Israel is afraid of the effectiveness of the information that could reach the international public opinion.

Apparently the PNA (Palestinian national authority) has control of the city since 1995, but the reality is different since in the outskirts of the city there are several Israeli checkpoints that are responsible for the entry and leaving of people. To make matters worse, the Zionist soldiers move freely within the city, invoking routines of security. It should be recalled that Nablus is part of the West Bank, known internationally as the occupied territories by Israel in 1967.Every day when they have to go elsewhere outside Nablus to work or simply to make some diligence, must pass through several check- points both for leaving as when they want to return back to Nablus, the perception towards the Israeli occupation is a fact, regardless of how optimistic are its inhabitants. With more than 500 dead and 2000 wounded of the Intifada, unfortunately, has made the uncertainty and anxiety are mixed with the spirit of the people of Nablus that cling to the hope of seeing one day the checkpoints and Jewish settlements, dismantled.

By Kassem Asmar Castellanos

Hebron city (al-Khalil in Arabic) is located to the southeast of the West Bank and although 140,000 Palestinians live in the city, all the region of Hebron has 580,000 inhabitants taking into account the municipalities and the Palestinian villages that surround it. Hebron is considered the largest Palestinian city of the occupied territories. As in Nablus, this city is under permanent siege and surveillance of the occupying Israeli forces, also with curfew with military patrols crossing the city. Israel has a great appetite for appropriating Hebron city, claiming that religiously it belongs to them, same with what they did with the eastern part of Jerusalem after the occupation of 1967. Israel always wields religious reasons to be able to annex Palestinian territories. We must not forget that as well as Hebron and Jerusalem are of great importance to the Jewish people, in the same way are important to the Christian and Muslim worlds. It is simply unacceptable that the will of 20 million Jews, imposed over the will of 1000 million Muslims and 1500 million of Christians and Catholics.

The city was divided in two zones because of a massacre committed by a Jewish settler who lived in a settlement on the outskirts of the city, against Palestinians who were in a mosque, killing 29 people and leaving 100 others wounded. Therefore as result of this tragic incident, a city's part with 85,000 Palestinian inhabitants, remained under Palestinian administration but the absurd situation is that the other part of Hebron that houses 55,000 inhabitants, stayed under scrutiny of the Israeli army that is the occupying force, with the pretext of protecting 500 colonists from a settlement that is at the city entrance. This situation has forced many Palestinian merchants to leave their business in this place of Hebron, for the reason that Palestinians' mobility has too much restriction and it is not possible to keep up a business under those circumstances. The element that continues being absurd is that 500 Jewish colonists have more freedom than any of the 140,000 Palestinian inhabitants of Hebron that have to pass several positions of control or checkpoints when they want to leave or enter the city, something like being a prisoner in your own land.

By *Kassem Asmar Castellanos*

The Palestinians are forced to tolerate the Jewish settlers who live in illegal settlements at the city's entrance, since they frequently throw stones and other objects at the houses of the Palestinians so many Palestinians have opted to put nets in the courtyards in order to prevent physical damage. Who is going to prosecute or punish the Jewish settlers?

It must be clarified that following the massacre in mention, the Zionist military established several checkpoints in the city, becoming the only city in the Palestinian territories that has inside the Palestinian community, military checkpoints. So if a Palestinian wants to go to a store or a pharmacy, it is probable that must stop at a check-point. It is not surprising to see Jewish colonists with soldiers wander the town, in front of the powerless eyes of its Palestinian inhabitants. Although Hebron is very important for all religions, I shall not go into detail on this topic. What I want to highlight is that the Palestinians of Hebron, have lived along centuries there, it would be completely illogical and irrational that the Zionists, in the blink of an eye seek to change the course of history with the argument "Divine Mandate", that the Palestinian territories belong to them. Obviously, Israel wants to put into its political context, religious reasons as an excuse to continue the expansionist ideology of the Zionist vision, taking as a basis the Jewish fundamentalism.

There are several settlements with their respective Jewish colonists in the outskirts of Hebron and all of them preach the same slogan, "Hebron city belongs to the Jewish people and Palestinians are unnecessary." That slogan from the perspective of the Zionist fundamentalists is shared with the ideology of the Israeli State.

It is not surprising that the West Bank, as soon as it was under the domain of the Israeli invasion, this region was subjugated to a fast policy of colonization that extended in all the occupied territories of West Bank and Gaza, even the Golan Heights of the Syrians, it could not be the exception. The fanaticism of Jewish and Zionist fundamentalism are extremely dangerous because they see the Jewish race as superior, with right to use all means to see all Palestine free from Arab Muslim and Christian. According to its prospects, the only ones who have the right to live in these lands are the Jews. Indeed, the Zionist extremist who committed the

By Kassem Asmar Castellanos

massacre against the Palestinians of Hebron, called Baruch Goldstein, his grave became a sort of pilgrimage for many of the colonists who visit it. And to think that this is happening in the 21th century but it is the truth, because there is nothing worse than the absolute unreasonableness which encloses the fanaticism and religious fundamentalism, regardless of its origin and is one of the most difficult obstacles, at taking part of any discussion or dialogue of peace.

Through fanaticism, its protagonists become irrational people who end up distorting the real course of events both current and historical. Any balanced mind rejects the argument of fundamentalists who say that it is legal and perfectly plausible, to expel and kill everyone that being in Palestine (mentioned as Israel) and not being Jewish, it is permitted by God through the Holy Scriptures of the Old Testament. This type of biblical stories so grossly distorted by those fanatical rabbis, don't have even the slightest dose of logic and rationality, especially if we take into account that the same tomb of the Patriarchs is a sacred place for both Jews and Muslims. Therefore, if those are the arguments and reasons that it will expose by the Israeli representatives in the peace talks, that means the peace is too far because already from beforehand is understood what the State of Israel wants, which is the invading force in the occupied territories of the West Bank, it is the peace but at the same time the West Bank.

In Hebron, from a purely demographic perspective, the Palestinians were always majority, as it can see in the statistics from the beginning of the 20th century. In 1905 the city had 15,000 inhabitants but 10% were Jews and the rest, Palestinians. Despite the pressures exerted by Israel with its army since they occupied the city in 1967, the Palestinians are still the vast majority. However, the Palestinians in this historic city are worried because there are many Jewish settlements in the outskirts of the city and there is one that it stands out, that is the Qiryat Arba settlement with a population of 8,000 settlers.

Since that bloody episode that headlined the radical colonist Goldstein, the city stayed semi-paralyzed because of was divided to protect about 500 Jewish colonists, but also it paralyzed a part of trade that is next to the Jewish colony because no Palestinian dares to open his business there and prefer leaving them. Most significant routes of Hebron have a beginning and an end to Palestinians because the checkpoints stationed there prevent that the Palestinians reach any place in Hebron. It sounds very absurd, that for the safety of a few illegal colonists, Israel has submited nearly 150,000 Palestinian inhabitants of the city of Hebron. There is no doubt that what tells us the former President Jimmy Carter in his book "Palestine: peace and not apartheid" refers precisely to those facts and incidents and the only thing that obtain is to create more hatred and resentment.

The attitude of the soldiers, together with the Jewish colonists in the heart of Hebron, converge to a constant goal which is scaring the Palestinians and if is possible force them to leave the city. Therefore, Palestinians who had business near Jewish colonists, moved to another area where they feel safer and there is the impression that the main aim of the Jewish settlements around Hebron, is to take over gradually the city. The arrogance of the Jewish settlers who assume defiant attitudes against the Palestinians under the protection of Israeli soldiers so, the Zionist army shows indifference because according to them, they have no faculty to intervene in those kinds of "events without importance".

Palestinians in this city survive thanks to an economic activity rather limited as are the cultivation of grapes, works of pottery, glass crafts, and its most important activity within the city is related with a well-known dairy products factory called "Al - Juneidi", although many residents have to go to other places of the occupied territories and Israel to seek a job and for working. Also, they have to face a difficult journey through many checkpoints.

Bethlehem (in Arabic Bet-lahem), It is a city with a lot of spiritual and religious air that receives tourists from many parts of abroad. Although Bethlehem's regions has 190,000 inhabitants represented in towns and villages scattered in an area of 620 km2. This religious city that is known by the name of Bethlehem has approximately 30,000 inhabitants where half are Christians and the other half profess the Muslim religion but have lived together for centuries and they have very clear that the problem which affects the normal development of their lives is the Israeli occupation.

By Kassem Asmar Castellanos

It is important to point out that Bethlehem, like other regions that make up the occupied territories which are: the area of Qalqilya, Salfit, Ramallah, East Jerusalem, Jenin, Tulkarm, Jericho, Nablus and Hebron, are surrounded by municipalities and small rural villages but the major problem, as it is the case with all the regions of the occupied territories, is the fragmentation of this territorial division because there are 22 Jewish settlements surrounding this important area and means that the Palestinians of this part of West Bank, should interrupt their mobility because of the checkpoints that are near the Jewish settlements and that makes the Palestinians can't approach too much. Describing it in another way, the Palestinians must walk with their minds activated all times to avoid misfortune, especially because the colonists are well-armed. It is important to recall that there are more than 150 Jewish settlements in the occupied territories.

The biblical narrations refer to this site as the home where our lord Jesus Christ was born and for the Jews is also important since King David was born and crowned in this place. By being part of the occupied territories in 1967, Bethlehem has been under subjugation of the Israeli occupation forces and although on paper, was transferred to the PNA (Palestinian national authority) in 1995, the Israelis don't need permission to get in and leaving the city the times that they want, since it is enough that they hold the slogan "for security reasons" and automatically becomes a personal consent for their soldiers, who end up patrolling the streets of Bethlehem.

As in Nablus and Hebron, Bethlehem is not the exception, since this small town is largely bordered by the security wall and many check-points. Jerusalem can be seen from Bethlehem because the only thing that separates them is just nine kilometers.

It is possible to feel a true spirit of Christmas in Bethlehem, with all the Majesty which characterizes this religious and ancient city. The Basilica of the Nativity considered an important bastion for the Christian faith because it is believed that it was erected in the same place where was born the Envoy of God, Jesus of Nazareth. The first stone that began to fit for the lifting of that Christian temple belongs the 4th century and therefore, it is considered the oldest Basilica in the Christianity world. Indeed, half of the Palestinians who live in Bethlehem are Christians but both

By Kassem Asmar Castellanos

Christians and Muslims coexist in harmony. The Basilica of the Nativity suffered a shameful Israeli military siege when 40 armed Palestinians entered there, to protect themselves from the persecution of the Zionist military.

Recently, UNESCO declared "Patrimony of humanity" the old part of Bethlehem and the Basilica of the Nativity. Can you guess who protested against this measure? Israel and the United States. The reason of the Israeli preoccupation is because once this small city was declared World Heritage, Israel is in the obligation, as occupying force, to respect the historical and cultural city sites, but what most concerns Israel is that the international community realizes the hostile policies and discrimination towards the Palestinian people and obviously about this topic, Israel has always kept total secrecy to prevent any possibility that the outside world know what is happening in the occupied territories. The proof is that foreigners who go to Israel or the occupied territories for reasons of tourism or other reasons, the Zionist authorities do whatever is within their reach, to convince them about the places that should visit, avoiding the populations that are inhabited by Palestinians in the occupied territories such as; Ramallah, Nablus, Bethlehem, Hebron, the East of Jerusalem, Jenin, among others. Israel has always tried to project the image of "the small country that defends itself from the Arab aggressors", as strategic measure to get the solidarity of the world public opinion, but on this issue, things have been changing for the simple reason that every time there are more people willing to go to the places where the Palestinians live under the Israeli occupation because many foreigners have realized the great deception that has tried to keep the Zionist system over decades.

The small religious town has on its periphery, Jewish colonists in settlements and being very near to Jerusalem; this area has become the biggest concentration of Jews settlers of all Palestine. We are talking about 350,000 colonists who have focused on places where the Palestinians have lived for many decades. This systematic process began in 1967, and despite the continual protests of the international community, the issue has turned in only protests. Settlements in this area have imposed a severe restriction on those peasants who have helped their families with their jobs for decades, related with agriculture and grazing herds

By Kassem Asmar Castellanos

because of the confiscation of lands (to be exact, theft of lands), restrictions on mobility and the theft of water by Israel in different way, among them we have to mention, extraction of this precious liquid, from the Palestinian subsoil. Obviously, this conclusion leads us to a frightening fact because time plays in favor of Israel, since their policies of discrimination and plunder of land against Palestinians, got worse with the passage of time. We don't need but to see the exponential course of the events, in the occupied territories since 1967 and anyone can realize that the vision and mission of Zionist movements, is being fulfilled with the complicity of the passive gaze of the international community that only limit to read isolated statements, condemning Israel but practically doesn't mean anything.

Bethlehem has been linked with Jerusalem by religious events that have historically occurred in those lands, but as a result of the wall's construction throughout the occupied territories in the West Bank, Jerusalem has been completely divided and separated from Bethlehem. Although it sounds easy the nine kilometers separating it from Jerusalem, in practice it is not so easy to get there. The Israeli measure of separating those important religious places has changed sensitively a physiognomy that was preserved for many centuries and the same thing happens with Hebron.

It is pertinent to clarify that today the Bethlehem area is smaller compared to what it was before the Israeli occupation in 1967, due to that Israel had annexed that same year, a part that was to the North of this small religious town. It was clear that Israeli expansionist policy was reflected from the same moment of the occupation, with a systematic territorial theft and since then they have not stopped of confiscating Palestinian lands and instead raise Jewish settlements to receive the Jews coming from different places of Europe and America. Entire Palestinian villages that remained on the outskirts of Bethlehem and its agricultural and grazing activities were considered a tradition, inherited from generation to generation that covered many decades, were literally severed and reduced to half its extension. To mention some of those villages, also known for its long agricultural history, we have Khader and Beit Jala known for its olive trees. Obviously that the aim of this land confiscations by the Apartheid regime in

118

By Kassem Asmar Castellanos

Israel, is the same common aim that has been applied in all corners of the occupied territories, in order to continue expanding illegal settlements.

If this wasn't enough, Israel followed annexing territories belonging to Bethlehem after taking advantage of the path of the wall that built because get in Bethlehem, and those lands that were on the other side of the wall, a part stayed in the hands of Israel. However, to reach a specific part of Bethlehem, can do it only those Palestinians who carry special permits at fixed hours and which prove that their purposes are to work the land, which is equivalent to say that any citizen in any place of the world has to ask for permission, permanently, to go to his house. Although many families of Bethlehem get their sustenance from the olives and olive oil, with the lifting of the separation wall many olive trees were destroyed and if we add the lands that stayed on the other side of this huge barrier, more the lands that Israel confiscated to build settlements for the Jewish settlers, all this situation makes that Palestinians have enough reason to feel worried, especially because the support to them from the international community does not go beyond a simple verbal condemnation to Israel, therefore this has not meant a shift in the systematic policy of expansionism and colonization of the occupied territories. However, in recent years in an hypocritical way, Israel definitely has expanded both the number of its settlements and the Jewish settlers in the occupied territories while at the same time participates in the peace talks with the Palestinians and that cynicism is being shared with its main ally and supplier of sophisticated weapons and financial resources that is the United States.

For the economy of Bethlehem, the decrease of tourists has been simply dramatic for this small town because of the wall gives the feeling that visitors are going to go to another country, moreover the check-points give that such impression. This situation has worsened life quality in many of its inhabitants who are part of the statistics of the unemployed Palestinians. If we consider that tourism is involved in an important part of income that Palestinians receives from Bethlehem, clarifying that this activity has decreased and if we add the restriction that Palestinians have for their mobilization, the Outlook is not so encouraging. All these

By *Kassem Asmar Castellanos*

events and circumstances have affected many businesses, that were among Arab populations on the periphery of this city, and have had to close because the wall extends the journey and the discomfort that cause the check-points add more difficulty to those who want to move from one side to another.

Qalqilya as well as many cities and areas of the West Bank, is a region where most of the people have links with farming activities. It is near the Mediterranean Sea and the number of its inhabitants is 50,000 but adding towns and municipalities belonging to its jurisdiction, reach about 110,000 inhabitants. This city shares the same phenomenon with the rest of the cities in the occupied territories due to the fact that also is surrounded by Jewish settlements. Given this circumstance, Israel entered into Qalqilya territory when decided to lift the separation wall with the shameless argument that it was a right of Israel to protect its settlers who are on Palestinian soil. As commonly happens in the West Bank, villagers have to walk as if they were living in a city full of labyrinths. On the one hand, the Palestinians have to avoid the Jewish settlements by the rules imposed by this racist system that builds roads for exclusive use of Jewish colonists belonging to those settlements, which means that Palestinians cannot go near. But If it wasn't enough, the separation wall has transformed Qalqilya and its surrounding municipalities in isolated cantons from the rest of the Palestinian territories which has hindered the life of many Palestinians in this region, especially at the time of traveling by the obstacles that are in the different check-points or positions of control that make Palestinians spend much time when they want to go to work, to study or for any other personal formality where necessarily must go through those sites of control.

Qalqilya, for having taken part actively in the second Intifada in 2000 that occurred as a result of the visit of the Israeli Prime Minister Ariel Sharon to the religious Muslims places, close the Al-Aqsa Mosque and the dome of the rock, which it was interpreted by the Palestinians as a direct provocation by the Executive Chief of Israeli government and if we add the own difficult conditions of the Palestinians because of Zionist occupation, this inevitably led at the start of the second Intifada. As always, the number of victims on the Palestinian side was a lot higher than the Israeli.

Israel, since then, has subdued strongly this city, controlling the movements of its inhabitants and building more Jewish settlements. Considering Qalqilya, as an area of high unemployment rate, are difficult the circumstances in which the inhabitants are. An unfortunate fact has happened with the trash and rubbish from Jewish settlements around Qalqilya, because of the settlers throw it toward the region where are the Palestinians, creating a problem of environmental pollution against the Palestinians.

It must be clarified that many Palestinian farmers in Qalqilya that have to go to work on their lands behind the wall, due to the fact that Israel built the wall of separation beyond the green line border. This made that agricultural land belonging to the Palestinians remain on the other side and there begin the persistent discomforts for the Palestinian farmers who have to reach their farmland through the check-points with special permissions, taking into account schedules routine imposed by the occupying forces. Nothing will change while the invading Israel forces do not withdraw their soldiers from the occupied territories.

While I was writing this book, I had the chance to read the content of a newspaper dated April 22, 2013 that said the following: "U.S. defense secretary Chuck Hagel said that the United States will give Israel advance missiles and a radar system for fighter aircraft, in order to continue ensuring the superiority and advantage of the Israeli air force over other countries in the region". What forgot to say the American Minister is that these huge financial and military aids to the State of Israel and that has kept for more than 65 years, i.e. Since 1948, has meant for Israel, green light to comply with the program of the expansionism of Zionist movements ideology, whose disastrous result has been a total control on all the Palestinian territories, with the implementation of policies of Apartheid, with a disgraceful content of racist and discriminatory rules against Palestinians, expelling its inhabitants who are the legitimate owners of these lands and in their place to build settlements, in order to receive Jews from different countries of the world and that are their homes and not the Palestinian territories. So the misfortune of the Palestinian people along many decades is due to the plot orchestrated by Israel and its partner and mentor that is the United States. Unfortunately,

By Kassem Asmar Castellanos

International community reaction has never been at the level of these events.

Jenin is part of the West Bank and is to the North of those territories. This town of about 37,000 inhabitants is mainly agricultural and it is next to a Palestinian refugee camp that has 13,000 inhabitants and dating back to 1953. They are refugees who were expelled by Israel in 1948. Jenin's area has 285,000 inhabitants between municipalities and towns on its periphery. Due to the fact that this city was active in the second Intifada, Israel as usual attacked ruthlessly this small town with tanks and helicopter gunships, demolishing many houses and imprisoning many Palestinians for having been part of the Intifada, which was a protest against Israeli occupation and its discriminatory policies against the Palestinians. The International community never realized the true statistics about the deaths that left this criminal incursion against the Palestinians because Israel prevented any presence of missions or foreign reporters in order to avoid that they discover this shameful and criminal practice in the occupied territory. Hundreds of homes were destroyed in that fateful year of 2012 when Israel attacked by land and air, didn't do it by sea because Jenin has no coast, otherwise, its warships would have participated too. At the end of the criminal siege, that lasted twelve days, the result could not be different because the destruction was reflected in a bleak panorama and in the disconcerted look of thousands of inhabitants of Jenin, nor health institutions were saved from this coward attack of Israel. The massacre was more than evident and intentional and the Israeli snipers seemed as if they were in an Olympic competition since they were shooting at anyone that moved; man, woman, boy or girl.

Israeli Prime Minister Sharon showed once again his hatred towards the Palestinians, not only destroying their homes, but also showing his true criminal side, by his contempt toward the lives of Palestinians. This situation could be observed when he sent his soldiers to assassinate many defenseless inhabitants. This dark figure that embodied the expansionist ideology of Zionism was required by a court in Belgium to answer a questionnaire about the genocide in the refugee camps of Sabra and Shatila in Lebanon where hundreds of defenseless Palestinians were massacred.

By Kassem Asmar Castellanos

United Nations' dignity was severely trampled by Ariel Sharon's Government, when Israel prohibited the presence in Jenin of a Commission designated by the Secretary General of the UN Kofi Annan to investigate the massacre in Jenin. The Israeli arrogant response was evident when he wanted by all the means to conceal the truth of barbarism perpetrated against the Palestinian people. As usually happens, the United States that always puts its cry in the sky when there's a massacre in any part of the world, did not even, spoke out about the Israeli mockery to the demands of the United Nations. Cynically, when Kofi Annan reacted to that refusal, Sharon with a pathetic style said that his country "had nothing to hide". Finally, Israel said that it would allow the presence of that Committee when their conditions that had been written by the Government of Ariel Sharón, "were respected". By the shameless of its content, which means for the international community, I will mention some of them:

(a) The evidence and documents required by the UN Commission would be supplied only by the authorities of Israel and not by another authority.

(b) This Commission would give assurance that no Israeli military would be judged for war crimes therefore, there would be no place to investigate the Israeli army.

(c) The witnesses that the UN Commission will interview should be chosen by Israel.

(d) Once the UN Commission ends its duty, refrain from writing its own conclusions.

Before the mocking posture of Israel, Kofi Annan understood that it was impossible for the Commission to do a serious job and for history the UN received a slap in its face from Israel, with the blessing of American government. Obviously as usual, due to the United States collaboration that permanently protects the criminal policy and expansionism of the Zionist State. Therefore, the international community could not condemn Israel for resisting to cooperate with the United Nations. Days later, potential witnesses had stated that Israel made efforts to hide evidence of the crimes that had committed in Jenin, burying many corpses in mass graves. If Zionists could hide the previous evidence, how was going Israel hide hundreds of destroyed homes? The bleak picture that the Zionist military incursion had caused, in fact it speaks by its self and Israel was so worried that the international community will come to know what had happened in Jenin that opted not to allow presence of any Commission that any international body had the intention of sending. Even, was not allowed the entry of any foreign media that had the purpose to visit the scene of the crimes.

Photo 6 Source AFP. "Image of the second Intifada"

A surprising fact that filled the Palestinians with pain and anger is that while the international community intervened in Kosovo, accusing the Serbian President Milosevic of war crimes, in the occupied territories Prime Minister Ariel Sharon had perpetrated crimes worse than those committed by Milosevic, obviously under the protection of the U.S. President George Bush, who was never tired of sharing smiles with his great ally Sharon, exchanging view-points about the peace process with the Palestinians. There is no doubt that these views' content was teeming with deceit and hypocrisy.

By Kassem Asmar Castellanos

With the advancement of technology through the Internet and advanced cell phones, nowadays it is difficult to hide information and events. Amnesty International in a discreet way had already collected data of the atrocities that the Israeli soldiers had committed in Jenin since it had clear evidence of many bodies that were buried among the ruins of the houses and in addition, Amnesty International reported that the soldiers fired without respect and if it wasn't enough, civilians could not leave the area during the siege. Therefore, there was a flagrant violation of human rights. A prominent member of Human Rights Watch, Peter Bauckaert said there were injured people who died waiting for medical care that never arrived because of the Israeli army refused to allow the passage of any ambulance or medical staff. This same agency said that Israel's violent incursion destroyed 600 houses of humble people in the refugee camp, however its inhabitants are reluctant to leave the area and since 1953 have suffered hostilities and humiliations. What maintains them on the edge of the resistance against the occupation forces is their unshakable conviction that their cause is just, very fair and as Jenin inhabitant said, "even if we have to continue enduring these hostilities and attacks, we do not lose hope that one day we will achieve the peace and independence for good of the future generations".

Although, the problem is not with the Jewish people but with the criminal policies of Apartheid, that the State of Israel practices and this is one of the main obstacles that it does not allow to reach an agreement with Palestinians.

Jerusalem is an ancient city of great religious importance to the three monotheistic religions that are; the Jewish, Muslim and Christian. After the first war between the recent Israel and the Arabs in 1948, was divided in two parts, the Western for the Jews and the eastern part for Palestinians under administration of Jordan. In the war of 1967 Israel occupied the West Bank, Gaza, Sinai and the Golan Heights. As East Jerusalem is part of the West Bank, remained under Israeli occupation and arbitrarily, Israel unified this city in 1980 and proclaimed it as the capital of Israel. The international community condemned this fact and the UN decreed the Resolution 478 that considered illegal and unacceptable the Israeli measure. With more than 150 illegal Jews settlements, scattered throughout the occupied territories, are the two issues more difficult to resolve in the peace talks with the Palestinians, due to the Israeli intransigence to assume a serious posture that means progress in the search of practical solutions for the two issues mentioned above.

In 1947, a Special Committee of the United Nations proposed that the city was divided in two, a part of the city for Jews and another part for Palestinians, although the Administration would be under a special regime of the United Nations. The proposal was accepted by Zionist leaders but not by Palestinians for the simple reason that being the Palestinians a majority, it was granting to the Jews one larger part of Jerusalem city. In the same way it happened with the rest of Palestine whose partition showed very clearly that it was favoring the Jews, especially if we take into account the United States arrogance in how they handled the situation from the United Nations, in order to incline the balance to favor the ideological cause of Zionists at the expense of the Palestinian people.

In the 1948 Arab-Israeli war, about 70,000 Palestinians were expelled from Jerusalem and its periphery and plunder was the agenda of the day. The Israeli authorities announced in a very particular way, that the business and homes of the Palestinians that "had abandoned the city" amounted 10,000 properties, simply passed into the hands of the Jews because according to Israel, it was violating a law that gave special powers to the Zionist Government to transfer these "abandoned" properties to the Israeli State.

David Ben Gurion, radical Zionist whose religious vision and his particular way of interpreting it, which "gave the right to Israel to seize every inch of the Palestinian territories" and he had no trouble as Prime Minister, to declare West of Jerusalem as part of Israel at the beginning of 1949. The international community reacted, refusing this illegal measure. In the 1967 war, Israel seized all Jerusalem when occupied the East part of Jerusalem and the most cynical and racist measures that began to implement, while all Jerusalem was under occupation Israeli military, consisted the Judaization of the city, evicting many Palestinians. Zionist laws were approved, that "allowed them" to go beyond the limits that Jerusalem municipality had before the war.

The annexation of East Jerusalem after the 1967 war, not only it limited to the Holy City, since Israel annexed 28 villages of the periphery and they joined them to Jerusalem, i.e. it was extended by adding 70 kms2 of Palestinian territory between East Jerusalem and the bordering towns of West Bank. Once the UN realized this practice, it was promulgated the Resolution 2253 by the General Assembly of the United Nations which demanded Israel to stop all its illegal initiatives for not altering the geographic and demographic composition of Jerusalem. In response, Israel not only disobeyed the UN Resolution but accelerated the confiscation of Palestinian lands and the expulsion of its inhabitants. The United States, as a sign of friendship with Israel, closed its eyes and did not condemn those facts. The Fourth Geneva Convention is clear in its content because flatly prohibits to any State that appropriates territory by military action to declare these lands as a part of the territory of the occupying power, therefore East Jerusalem's annexation is totally unacceptable.

Another law of Apartheid policy that Israel had promulgated a long time ago, that leaves no doubt about racist measures against the Palestinians, has to do with a set of rules that decreed Israel in 1967, about the Palestinian inhabitants of Israel where they were faced with a difficult dilemma that consisted to accept Israeli citizenship or a kind of "permanent residence" in Jerusalem. Many Palestinians saw that acceptance of Israeli citizenship was as a contribution to their plans (Zionist plans) to "legalize the Israeli occupation". The problem with those who decided to accept the "permanent residence" that were the majority is that they must continue living in Jerusalem and if they decide to travel, it should be for short periods. Long absences may give the faculty to Israel to revoke or abolish their "permanent residence" in Jerusalem. They cannot even go and live for a relatively long period with a family member that is found elsewhere in the occupied territories. While the Jews who want to leave the holy city the time wishing, the gates not only of Jerusalem but anywhere of the occupied territories, they will always find them open, due to the "kindness" of the occupying forces.

By Kassem Asmar Castellanos

We don't have to be experts in International Affairs to reach the conclusion that it is a discriminatory measure that seeks to reduce the Palestinian presence in Jerusalem, to comply with the main purpose of Judaizing the city.

Another important aspect has to do with the route of the separation wall (Israel calls it the security wall) where were confiscated 19% of lands of humble Palestinians from Jerusalem. In this sense, the international community had pronounced and the Security Council of the United Nations in 1968 through the Resolution 252 reminded Israel what had said the Resolution 2253 of 1967. This new Resolution clarified to Israel the illegality and invalidity of all its measures that have as goal, expropriate and expel Palestinians with the dark purpose of changing the geographic and demographic aspect of Jerusalem. Israel since took control of all Jerusalem in 1967, its pretention was always to Judaize the city, by applying discriminatory rules against the Palestinians to change the population facet in Jerusalem with political and expansionism purposes, additionally to reduce the Palestinian identity in the city.

This Zionist strategy that has been implemented with the complicity of the American Governments, it has allowed Israel to carry out a sequential colonization policy on a large-scale with the construction of many settlements in East Jerusalem belonging to Palestinians and on the periphery of the city where Jerusalem is surrounded by Jewish neighborhoods and settlements that are on the Palestinian side. Therefore, the racist State of Israel has received more than 220,000 Jewish settlers that added with the 330,000 who live in other settlements in the rest of the occupied territories, we can say that there are more than 550,000 Jews in illegal settlements in the occupied territories. Furthermore, in East Jerusalem as in any other place in the occupied territories, if a Palestinian wants to build a house, he has to get a special permission from Zionist authorities and the occupying forces which means a bureaucratic process and in most of time, expensive and quite cumbersome. Those Palestinians who build without permission, their homes can be demolished. So pathetic situation, ask for permission to the usurpers and the occupying forces to build!

By Kassem Asmar Castellanos

The following information reflects the size of the Zionist expansion in East Jerusalem, annexed by Israel. The policy of expansionism and Judaization of Jerusalem at great rate is reflected in the more than 50,000 houses that have been built in the eastern part of the city that has allowed them illegally to welcome to more than 220,000 Jews from many parts of the world and this has been possible with the expulsion of many Palestinians and the demolition of their houses. But in contrast, the Palestinians could only build 800 houses in the same lapse of time and the reason is that for a Palestinian get a permit or license to build his home, it is a real titanic task. Another measure of racial segregation is one that has to do with regulations issued by Israel against the Palestinian inhabitants of Jerusalem to become a psychological dissuasive power, with the aim to force them to leave the city to restrict the number of Palestinian inhabitants in Jerusalem. For example, a Palestinian who is married with another Palestinian but is not from Jerusalem, cannot take his wife or her husband to live in Jerusalem, in spite of that is Palestinian land. The same thing happens when someone wants to take his child. Obviously, the purpose of this racist measure is to force many Palestinians to renounce their rights to live in Jerusalem. We must not forget that there is a parallel law, which removes the right of residence of Palestinians in Jerusalem when they are absent a relatively long period. Now suppose if a citizen or a Palestinian family that has to stay one or two years out of Jerusalem and at the end of that time takes the determination of returning, in practice it will be difficult due to discriminatory policies of housing, that makes always, a constant lack of housing for the Palestinian population of Jerusalem.

So strong is the Judaization that Jerusalem has suffered, that those Palestinians who live in just two or three kilometers from the city, have to get a special permit for specific time to enter the city. This situation generates a bitter taste among Palestinians who ask themselves how is it possible that Palestinians who have lived in that region for centuries and through many generations, have to stop in each place to ask for permission of limited time for going from one place to another on their own territory, while European Jewish colonists who have so little time living in the occupied territory that can be counted with the fingers of a hand have more freedom in the West bank and in Jerusalem.

By Kassem Asmar Castellanos

The report of the ACRI (Association for civil rights in Israel) from mid-2012 ensures that ¾ parts of East Jerusalem's Palestinian population live in poverty. Unfortunately, the treatment, which receives about 320,000 Palestinians by the Zionist authorities of Jerusalem, is diametrically opposite to the special treatment that West Jerusalem and Jewish colonists who live in the settlements and illegal neighborhoods in East Jerusalem have. The Palestinians situation got worse when Israel lifted the separation wall, which meant the disunity with the rest of the occupied West Bank, so it has become very difficult to reach Jerusalem and has forced that many Palestinians from the rest of the West Bank, limit significantly their visits to Jerusalem which has resulted in a situation of closing of many business that Palestinians have had for decades. The situation of the Palestinians is simply very difficult and in this sense we should be objective since this is an abusive measure and racist tactic of the occupation forces, which seek to despair and intimidate the spirit of struggle of the Palestinians in all corners of the occupied territories in order to force them to abandon what have been their homes for centuries.

By Kassem Asmar Castellanos

8. THE JEWISH'S LOBBY AND THE UNITED NATIONS IN THE ISRAELI-PALESTINIAN CONFLICT

We often see and hear a repeated term, especially at election times in the United States and many people are not able to understand the magnitude of its content. I am referring to the "Jewish Lobby".

The term "Jewish or Zionist Lobby", it refers to the domain of a significant segment of the American Jewish community that has a broad power to unify criteria through its associations and agencies seeking the direction in which they believe necessary for the foreign policy of the United States, which should be a guarantee for the interests of Israel. Even in times of elections in the United States, because of Jews have control above an important sector of the media; they can influence the outcome of the elections. They also have the strategic ability of sponsoring any campaign, making donations of millions of dollars for one specific presidential candidate who could be better for the interests of the Zionist State. How is it possible that a relatively small number of Jewish communities achieve this?

Its ability is such that they have reached to permeate several Christian organizations to get their respective supports before the public opinion. Indeed, in many occasions we see leaders and Christian pastors talking about Israel wonders, in their special television and radio programs, which are aimed to many countries worldwide. The Jewish lobby maintains special control in the U.S. Congress with the objective to guarantee permanent economic support and huge political and military support for Israel. Even, there are Christian leaders with strong influence in the U.S. Congress as Dick Armey that being Christian, defends as an inveterate radical Zionist, the Israeli interests. But the Jewish lobby is not limited to the explanations given above since they also have presence in important technological and financial sectors.

By Kassem Asmar Castellanos

U.S. financial aid to Israel exceeds 3500 million dollars a year and the Jewish lobby has achieved that the United States doesn't check how Israel spends these monetary resources. For example, a part of the U.S. aid is used to Israeli expansionism, building more settlements for the Jewish settlers in the occupied territories. The Jewish lobby takes advantage of any aspect involving American society on the agenda of the Congress. For example, when President Bush declared war against terrorism at the end of 2001, Israel took advantage of this situation to express its deep understanding towards the United States since Israel was also harassed by two terrorist organizations as Hammas and Hezbollah. In this way, tries to legitimize crimes that Israel has perpetrated against Palestinians and the continuous massacres in Gaza. Additionally, Israel dedicates a special effort towards religious activities, where Israeli expansionism and Jewish settlements' construction as the endless occupation of the Palestinian territories, tries to justify it by saying that it is a legitimate right of "Divine Mandate", Although this absurd and misleading thesis has lost strength due to the fact that world public opinion has realized the atrocities against the Palestinian people and the non-compatibility of these behaviors with any of the Scriptures.

Freedom of speech which the United States, as a great nation defends it, accompanied with the imposing image of the Liberty´s statue, it is incompatible with the Jewish lobby. Who journalist dares to report the permanent Israeli abuses against Palestinians? Who dares to question the Israeli expansionist policy in the occupied territories, from its drafting office? Almost nobody for fear of being fired from their jobs.

The strongest Jewish Lobby in the United States is AIPAC (U.S.-Israeli public Affairs Committee), this Committee or Association closely monitors the foreign policy of the United States and its relationship with Israel, i.e., always ensures that the layout of American foreign policy, end up favoring the interests of Israel. One of its main objectives is to keep always, special interest from the United States Congress towards Israel and they do so during election campaigns where make a strong advertising campaign, providing considerable doses of money for those candidates to Congress who show their deep "affection" towards

By *Kassem Asmar Castellanos*

Israel and their willingness to support the Israeli policy in the occupied territories. AIPAC does not save the slightest effort to get approvals that considers necessary in the U.S. Congress to acquire huge financial aid, military and policies as permanent support for Israel. There is no doubt that all matters on the activities inherent to the Jewish lobby are mentioned very secretly in American society to avoid discomfort or commotion. Furthermore, the representative of the United States to the Security Council of the United Nations does not escape from the guidelines that are established by the Jewish lobby and leaders of Congress influenced by AIPAC.

The Secretary-General of the United Nations, on the paper, is called to do an objective and impartial job since he is the representative by excellence of the UN for the world and he should be a very high-profile diplomat to lead peace processes and additionally to propose solutions to any crises that could arise in different parts of the world in relation to political matters, economic and social issues, and also regarding human rights. His most important role is to give suggestions, which have direct relation with the stability of peace and with all delicate conflicts that could threaten countries or regions. He must have a wide availability to listen and analyze the representatives of the UN, in order to present their concerns before the United Nations and draw his own conclusion, but what is the UN? The UN (United Nations Organization) was set up in 1945 with the purpose of preserving peace and harmony among people, taking determinations that could consolidate the goals. Another of its objectives is to make efforts to resolve and prevent conflicts among countries, in addition, to promote multilateral cooperation in order to find proposals and solutions for issues of common interest such as economic matters and regards human rights.

There are several organs within the United Nations but I will mention two that interest us, the General Assembly and the Security Council. The UN General Assembly takes into account the participation of all its members who are 194 which represent same number of countries that have the right to use their respective votes. There, should be carried out discussions of different kinds and priorities, also speeches by several heads of

By Kassem Asmar Castellanos

States. Among the exercises that involve the General Assembly, is to make observations and recommendations about conflicts, famine, economic problems and development and to formulate initiatives related to the global warm up among other common goals. These discussions and exercises are given each year.

The Security Council of the United Nations, in contrast to the General Assembly has only 15 members, among them there are five who are permanent members; the United States, Russia, China, Great Britain and France. These countries were granted in 1945 the right to use a mechanism that gives them the power to block and leave without effect any initiative or draft Resolution on any issue about the security and peace, topics that are discussed in this organ and this mechanism is called the Veto.

The Resolutions, which may be approved in the enclosure of the UN Security Council, become dissuasive measures for a specific country or countries comply with its contents. The other 10 non-permanent members are elected by the General Assembly for two years, as members in the Security Council. Anyway, to vote any Resolution within the UN Security Council, it is necessary to keep in mind that there are 15 votes among their members. Never a country of the permanent members of the security Council had used the veto to protect the interests of a country as did it the United States where exercised the "right" to block Resolutions in 42 opportunities, Resolutions condemning Israel for its expansionism and discriminatory practices against the Palestinian people. Additionally, Israel has a large record, flouting dozens of UN Resolutions, asking many times to Israel to stop its policy of construction of settlements in the occupied territories, and to put an end to its discriminatory measures and violations of human rights against Palestinians and once and for all, Israel should withdraw their troops from the West Bank, East Jerusalem and the Golan Heights of Syria as prerequisite for a serious solution in the Middle East.

Since the UN was created, the Palestinian issue is which more has monopolized discussion and attention but also we have to say it, is the conflict where more irreverence have been shown by continuous American practice of using the veto in order to avoid any damning Resolution against Israel or because Israel does not respect international legality, comes from where it comes from.

By Kassem Asmar Castellanos

Throughout its history as a State, Israel in the last 65 years has eluded many times the outcry of the international community about the Israeli-Palestinian conflict. Unfortunately, both the United States and Israel conduct in this international organization are not compatible with the ethical and moral spirit of the UN, which tends to impart justice with equity, in order to keep and achieve peace and coexistence in harmony among the countries.

Without doubt, there is an agreement of understanding between the United States and Israel where its unwavering solidarity and mutual alliances has meant in the last 65 years, a disastrous damage against the Palestinian aspirations that seek to achieve his self-determination. The President of the Palestinian National Authority, Mahmud Abbas said recently in the main precinct of the United Nations that the Palestinians are only claiming 22% of what was Palestine until the mid-20th century to set up their State. Is this too much to ask for?

By *Kassem Asmar Castellanos*

9. PALESTINIAN-ISRAELI PEACE PROCESS: MORE THAN TWENTY YEARS OF DIALOGUE WITHOUT ANY IMPORTANT PROGRESS

Usually, the Israeli-Palestinian conflict is shown by Israel and the United States, as a conflict very complex and a very difficult issue to resolve that needs a special dose of patience and prolonged persistence. Well, this thesis is a false myth that several countries have invented to continue justifying the never-ending Israeli occupation of the territories of the West Bank, the Golan Heights and East Jerusalem. Moreover, to carry out another Zionist essential objective that is to plunder water resources. About this subject, we have to be direct in pointing out that it is absolutely false that the solution is complex. The main problem is that the solution they want to impose on the Palestinians, essentially drafted by any American administration of the White House that ends up helping its friend Israel and this is what has made any solution ends in failure.

It is imperative to clarify that the claims of the Palestinian people has been reduced to a minimum of 22% of all the Palestinian territory which there was until mid-20th century and it is obvious that Palestinians must remain immovable at this point, otherwise it would be giving all the lands of Palestine, that is precisely what the Zionist ideology always has wanted. Conclusion, those who have hampered the way towards a fair solution and a clear peace agreement and without guile, were Americans and Israelis with their proposals and plans of peace that is unacceptable by its lack of seriousness and common sense. More than 20 years have passed, since the first contacts and dialogues were taken between Israelis and Palestinians, no greater progress has been made and I am afraid that with the arrogance of Israel with its permanent tactic of trying to deceive the Palestinian people and the international community with the blessing of its main ally that is the United States, It is difficult to reach a peace agreement under circumstances, with visible absence of will and common sense. Another argument that continues being a huge farce is that Israel is used to show, concerning political organization Hammas (Israel considers it terrorist organization) to justify the little progress in negotiations of peace because of (according Israel) the attitude and policies of this group. About this Israeli lie, we should mention that Hammas won the Palestinian general elections in 2006, i.e. the dialogues of peace between the Palestinians and Israelis to date, had already passed more than 13 years and during all that period of time, Israel never showed willingness and serious commitment in these talks, even its arrogance and cynicism took such dimension because while the Zionists were talking about peace with Palestinians, simultaneously they were destroying and confiscating homes of Palestinians in order to continue building more settlements in the occupied territories. Meanwhile, the United States was regretting by Israeli attitude but at the same time, the Americans used the veto to block any Resolution of the Security Council of the United Nations that sought to condemn Israel for its blatant and illegal practices.

Another lie that Israel shows in its speech is when tries to argue that the problem of the Middle East has a religious nature (according Israel) due to that the Arabs with a radical religious vision want to put an end to the existence of Israel. It should be noted that this hoax is even bigger than the earlier ones by the reason of Zionist ideology which was set 115 years ago, has a nature purely religious and expansionist because their leaders had come to the conclusion that all Palestine belongs to them and the only people with right to inhabit these lands are the Jews by "Divine Mandate" enshrined in the ancient writings. So, the equation concerning this last point has been completely reversed by Israel and which corroborates this fact is that Israel wants to keep up this deception to show as a legitimate right, tens of settlements that have been built in the last 45 years in the West Bank, East Jerusalem and the Golan Heights, where instills in its Israeli citizens that this expansionist practice has the unequivocal backing of the precepts contained in the biblical writings and who don't deserve to live in those territories are the Palestinians.

I visited the occupied territories in mid-2008 and I realized the sincere will of the majority of Palestinians in different places, to reach a peace agreement that allows them to live with the Jews free of hatred or resentment. This shows that the Palestinian people is a society that despite abuses, hostility and discrimination that have had to endure for so many years, they are willing to

By Kassem Asmar Castellanos

shake the hand of any Israeli citizen in order to share a true peaceful coexistence that take into account the rights of all the involved in this conflict. It is possible that someone questions what I said, recalling that from Gaza Hammas launches its Qassam rockets over Israel and that may contradict the peaceful spirit mentioned. The first thing that it needs to be clarified is that for many years, the inhabitants of the Gaza Strip have lived a strong Israeli military siege and blockade which literally strangled its economy in such a way that the poverty has increased dramatically and if we add to this the massacres because of the infernal Israeli military operations on Gaza, therefore, this ended up generating hatred and resentment.

It is not necessary to extend the comment about Gaza, because has been treated in a previous chapter, although it sounds somewhat strange, the best thing that could happen to Israel is that Hammas has won the elections because automatically this meant that Israel found a pretext to paralyze and avoid its commitment with the international community and with the dialogues and peace agreements, saying that a terrorist organization is ruling in the occupied territories and as if that was not enough , they took it as an excuse to expand its settlement network in the West Bank and in East Jerusalem, but the more surprising and shameful is that this practice, it began to do without any kind of discretion and before eyes of world public opinion and obviously their leaders, especially the main western countries led by the United States whose only and weak "reactions" were not more than gestures in favor of Israel, attempting to show that their Governments were concerned with the expansionist policy and building of settlements in the invaded territories, but that in reality it never meant a serious pressure against Israel, for the simple reason that were ephemeral and verbal sentences without any practical effect. In this sense, Israel never felt concern about these theoretical condemnations to such an extent that settlement constructions in the occupied Palestinian territories has remained constant from 1967 until today.

By Kassem Asmar Castellanos

The conclusion derived from this whole situation is that Western countries and especially the United States, have a high responsibility to be lenient with Israeli expansionist policy and the question we must ask is; did the international community do any significant effort to stop the Israeli expansionist policy in the occupied territories? The answer is no.

Years later, Western countries had kept always a same slogan in the sense that any solution to the Israeli-Palestinian conflict should be canalized through peace talks whose first requirement consisted that the representatives of the Palestinian people should recognize the right of Israel to exist. Palestinian leaders felt the need to bet on a mechanism that in their view could be more practical as a solution to the conflict and they communicated this desire to Western countries at the beginning of the 1990s. Palestinians decision produced much expectation not only on the Palestinian people but also in many regions around the world but with the passing of the years, the frustration and disappointment were the main elements in all meetings between Palestinians and Israelis, why?

I will outline the most important plans, agreements and dialogues for peace between Palestinians and Israelis which seen until now, never stop to be a total failure, according what it can be seen in the occupied territories.

♦ The first direct contacts between Arabs and Israelis occurred in 1977 when the Egyptian President, Anwar al-Sadat made a trip to Israel to propose a peace agreement between both countries. Though before that trip, the Arab countries had communicated to the Egyptian President their dissatisfaction by the determination which had taken, because of the Arabs saw that the only key for the crisis in the Middle East had to start from the basis of a widespread solution involving an Israeli commitment to a total withdrawal from all the territories that Israel occupied in 1967 and not as al-Sadat had outlined it in 1977, through isolated agreements that they didn't take into account the participation and the legitimate right of the Palestinians and Syrians of the occupied territories in the West Bank, the Gaza Strip and the Golan Heights respectively.

By Kassem Asmar Castellanos

The situation that weighed over the most populous Arab country and maybe the poorest, was one of the central reasons, that made President Sadat reflects to move closer to the West, and particularly to the United States through initiative of peace that honoring the truth, was limited to a minimal expression due to that they were discussing the return of Sinai to Egypt in Exchange for peace between Israel and Egypt and not with the Arab world.

While the top headlines of the world press had mentioned the Sadat's trip to Jerusalem at the end of 1977 as historical with his speech in the Knesset (Israeli Parliament), although that was an euphoric moment and not something relevant if we take into account the fundamental point of the Camp David agreement, was the desert of Sinai. The Israeli Prime Minister Menachem Begin, was always elusive on the issue of the Palestinian occupied territories, and even he remained more elusive at the moment to talk about Palestinian sovereignty although both Begin and al-Sadat had glimpsed the possibility to give to Palestinians, some autonomy in the Palestinian territories, but the mere fact that the Egyptian President tried to assume the representation of the Palestinian people, obviously caused much indignation in Arabic world and mainly among Palestinians.

Different interpretations have been given to Camp David's peace agreements between Israel and Egypt signed in 1979, in the sense that was the key to future peace talks but the truth is different because the winner of this diplomatic maneuver was Israel on having left its strongest opponent, in Exchange for a piece of desert and the rest of analysis only are speculations on the basis that shows us the outlook of the occupied territories in the 21th century, where the Palestinians situation cannot be more complicated and gloomy.

The conflict prolongation hurts more to the Palestinians than to the Israelis. According to the data handled by the Israeli NGO Bztselem (NGO), more than 5400 Palestinians and 480 Israeli died between 2000 and 2008 in this conflict, i.e., more than 90% of those who die in Israel and the occupied territories are Palestinians, Without forgetting the exaggerate increase of the settlements.

By Kassem Asmar Castellanos

♦ In October of 1991 began the peace conference in Madrid, with the presence of the leaders Mikhail Gorbachev of the Soviet Union, George Bush of the United States and high-level representatives of Palestine, Jordan, Syria, Lebanon, Israel, the Arab League and the European Union. Different kinds of meetings warmed the atmosphere when Israel and several Arab countries had accused each other. Although the Spanish press tried to give a larger dimension that its true meaning, this Conference produced much more expectation than any major achievement.

♦ For first time, the PLO (Palestine Liberation Organization) and Israel had reached an agreement of understanding sponsored by U.S. President Bill Clinton and this achievement was known as the 1993 Oslo accords. Palestinian leader Yasser Arafat and Israeli Prime Minister Isaac Rabin represented the antagonistic parties. Perhaps was the most decisive agreement between Israeli and Palestinian representatives but at the same time, had created controversy because of the amphibology of its content.

About this agreement, it has said that the Norwegian Government was the one that carried out most of the secret negotiations and that the United States only had to intervene to formalize it but many people have their doubts in the smallest role that Americans had "allegedly" contributed to consolidate those peace agreements. The formal commitment of this agreement was given with the mutual recognition of the highest representatives of both sides, i.e. the PLO with its main figure Yasser Arafat that expressed for first time the right of Israel existence and at the same time, the Israeli Prime Minister Isaac Rabin who recognized the PLO as the legitimate representative of the Palestinian people and the right of this people to self-determination. In short, the most important points of this agreement are as follows:

a) A gradual withdrawal from the Gaza Strip and West Bank of the Israeli troops and the temporary and provisional establishment of Palestinian Government, that later it would call PNA (Palestinian national authority) and Palestinian Council that represents Palestinians in the occupied territories, in a democratic way.

b) This transition will have a period of five years and after this, it will set up a permanent condition based to Resolutions 242 and 338 of the United Nations Security Council.

By Kassem Asmar Castellanos

c) The Palestinian national authority will have the right to exert its rule in the areas of education, culture, health and tourism.

d) Likewise, the Palestinians will develop a police institution to ensure order and security in the territories where are going to exert their authority.

e) Regarding the handling of matters related with electricity and water, the representatives of both sides are committed to reach an agreement. (until to date, there has not been any serious agreement on that point).

But the issue that most annoyed the encouragement of the Palestinian people is related to the Jewish settlements in the West Bank because in the Oslo agreements, were excluded from those talks. Same thing happened with the question of East Jerusalem, Palestinian refugees, and borders delimitation, though they hinted that in the future these issues could be debated to define once and for all its status. All this within the framework of the Resolutions mentioned above although the Israeli euphemism, flagrantly, assaulted the good faith that the Palestinian delegation had deposited in the agreements, on having believed in the commitment that Israel had assumed before Palestinians and the international community, especially concerning settlements and East Jerusalem. For the Palestinians, the issue of settlements is vital because without their dismantling it would be impossible to speak about the future Palestinian State and the damage which means for daily life of Palestinians, since Israel takes powers of "legitimate right", in order to use the road network belonging to the Jewish settlements to make sure the security of its settlers and if this it wasn't enough, the illegal exploitation agricultural and the excessive consumption of water coming out of the Palestinian territories.

These accords foresee that after the five years the Oslo agreement refers, based on Resolutions 242 and 338, Israel gives it particular interpretation, especially related to Resolution 242, in which way? Resolution 242 of 1967 of the UN Security Council establishes that no country can annex territories by force and therefore demands that Israel withdraws from territories that occupied during the war of 1967. The rights of all the countries in the regions, must be guaranteed to live in peace within secure

By Kassem Asmar Castellanos

and recognized borders. Those countries have to achieve a clear and fair agreement with the theme of refugees, and the free passage of navigation in international waters must be responsibility of both sides.

Israel has given singular interpretation to this Resolution that obviously helps them a lot to insinuate that the Resolution says that Israel must withdraw from occupied territories and does not specify that must withdraw from all occupied territories. In other words, being absent the article **the**, Israel automatically understands that it is not forced to withdraw from all the territories occupied in 1967, and therefore takes it as a "legitimate" measure to justify through peace negotiations a withdrawal according to its will, which automatically means crumbs of territories to the Palestinians and that is what has been happening with the Oslo agreement.

♦ In March of 2000, failed an endeavor of the United States through its President Bill Clinton, to convince the Syrian President of that time Hafez Al-Assad, to be part of a possible bilateral conversation with Israel for the issue of the Syrian Golan Heights which is under Israeli occupation since 1967. What has not allowed the takeoff of any dialogues between Syria and Israel with reference to this territory, basically because Israel insists that there should be no precondition for the start of such a dialogue, while Syria put as a condition that Israel commits itself publicly to return to Syria the Golan Heights, before starting any talk of peace. Who benefits with the absence of a peace agreement between Israel and Syria? Obviously Israel, which continues exploiting the fertile Golan Heights soil with its inhabitants living in illegal settlements, but the special benefit that represents the Golan Heights to Israel is that a significant part of the water that Israel consumes comes from this region, so while those talks continue being postponed, there is a clear beneficiary.

♦ In mid- 2000, The President of the United States Bill Clinton, wanted to revitalize the peace talks between Palestinians and Israelis, which were paralyzed in a dark path and whose outcome was not at all encouraging. The appointment was at Camp David, a ranch of presidential rest on the outskirts of Washington, and though since the start of these talks the images that showed the different media of the three leaders involved in these dialogues,

By Kassem Asmar Castellanos

with many handshakes, the crude reality was diametrically opposed because the most sensitive matters to be treated as the Jewish settlements and the issue of East Jerusalem, the Israeli delegation always evaded those important topics. Israel showed its unwavering desire to keep most of its network of settlements in the West Bank, and in return Israel offered a piece of territory near the Gaza Strip and in the Negev desert, of lower quality and size. In practical terms, Yasser Arafat could not accept the Israeli proposal because that condemns the Palestinian people to live in a broken and discontinuous territory into cantons. We must not forget that the settlements are scattered throughout the West Bank and have "jurisdiction" that prohibit to Palestinians to approach them as it also prohibits Palestinians, to use "their" road network and for common sense reasons, Yasser Arafat could not accept this proposal because it cannot be implemented a Palestinian State simply for being unworkable.

Another thorny topic is related to East Jerusalem where Israel through its Prime Minister Ehud Barak proposed that this part of the religious city could be administered jointly, but the Palestinian leader responded that he could not give up an important part of Palestinian sovereignty. These differences between both sides, led to failure of those dialogues that had an antecedent not so prominent, the 1993 Oslo agreement. Sincerely, the implementation of these agreements, from the beginning had ignored issues such as Jewish settlements and East Jerusalem, and necessarily it was going to end up in a vicious circle, therefore with this so murky scene, the American President wanted to any cost and before the end of his mandate, unlock the process of Arab-Israeli peace, arranging the meeting in camp David but this objective was impossible to achieve. At the end of the meeting and despite the pressure on Palestinian leader Yasser Arafat, he did not change his opinion because of the differences were large and not as days later said President Clinton, "the historic moment was squandered" by the Palestinian representatives.

Another Israeli argument is that it had never made so many concessions to Palestinians, although neither is true this reasoning because the word concession is not compatible with the occupied territory, since is Palestinian land that is under Israeli military occupation. After two weeks of meetings at Camp David,

By Kassem Asmar Castellanos

the two delegations left this place and President Clinton had to see the failure of this Summit.

It is very important to point out that Israeli Prime Minister Ehud Barak presented his proposals with a surprising coincidence with a strategic plan developed in 1967 by an Israeli politician named Yigal Allon, known as the "Allon Plan" and in which central points had suggested that Israel had to annex a large part of the territories that occupied in 1967 and allow the establishment of a Palestinian Government with limited functions in the rest of the West Bank and the Gaza Strip. In other words, 22% of what was Palestine until the middle of the 20th century and that is what Palestinians claim to constitute their State, but would be reduced to no more than 13% of the Palestinian territories, according to the proposal of Allon Plan. So, it would be nothing outlandish to say that the Israeli delegation took on its agenda to the Camp David summit, the old and ridiculous proposal of this Plan.

♦ In January 2001 it carried out in Taba, located in the Sinai Peninsula, some meetings between delegates from Israel and Palestine. This meeting was known with the name of the Taba Summit. At that Summit, Ehud Barak who was not there, due to his occupied agenda with the proximity of the elections in Israel, had made a series of proposals that did not actually contain substantive changes in comparison with all previous proposals. He repeated what the Palestinians did not want to hear, since Israel returned to suggest its intention of keeping most of Jewish settlements scattered in the West Bank and that the solution in relation to East Jerusalem could be solved taking into account the demographic situation of this part of the city, i.e., where there are Jews is annexed by Israel and the tiny part where are the Palestinians would be the future capital of a Palestinian State.

It is not necessary to have more than half a brain to understand that since 1967, were built many settlements and Jewish neighborhoods in East Jerusalem, where Israel has housed more than 220,000 Jews and additionally always the international community has considered them illegal. These practices violate the Fourth Geneva Convention and the Resolutions 446, 465, 298, 242, 252, 478 and 298 of the UN Security Council. In short, those Resolutions consider that these settlements have no legal support and they are a serious obstacle to reach a peace agreement between the parties. Moreover, the expropriations and confiscations of Palestinian lands and their inhabitant's displacement for such expansionist purpose, are totally unacceptable and illegal; therefore Israel is obliged to dismantle all the settlements in the occupied territories. In this order of ideas, the Palestinians cannot accept this kind of proposals for the simple reason that preclude the implementation of conditions for a future Palestinian State; otherwise, they would be legitimizing the illegal policies against its own people that have been rejected by the international laws according the above mentioned Resolutions. At the end of Taba Summit, it was not possible to celebrate anything, because there was not any important agreement between Israeli and Palestinian representatives.

♦ In February 2002, Saudi Arabia presented a global initiative for the pursuit of a peaceful solution in order to resolve the Arab-Israeli conflict and this initiative was named "Saudi Peace Plan". In its essence proposes normalization of relations at all levels between Israel and Arab countries in exchange, the Jewish State must withdraw its troops until the borders established immediately before the 1967 war. In this plan, was mentioned the Golan Heights of Syria, East Jerusalem, the West Bank and the Gaza Strip. Few hours later, the Israeli Prime Minister Ariel Sharon rejected this initiative but the most absurd fact that displayed Sharon, when said that he would like to meet Saudi leaders to talk about the issue. Immediately, a distinguished Egyptian personality warned Israel when said that Israel should not deceive, using traps with the Saudi Plan, focusing only on the aspect of relations with Arab countries, due to the crucial point are the occupied territories. In fact that Israel once he learned about the Saudi plan, proposed a meeting between diplomatic of both countries to normalize the relations between Saudi Arabia and Israel. Obviously, the Saudi reaction could not be different, because of the rejection to that Israeli insinuation was categorical.

♦ In 2003, a shared effort among the United States, Russia, the UN and the European Union in the search of a solution to the Israeli-Palestinian conflict, ended in the elaboration of a text called the "road map". As seen on previous occasions, this initiative aspired to propel the peace process between the two sides on the need to set up a Palestinian State but the question that remained unresolved was, under what conditions the American administration and the Israeli Government had conceived this Palestinian State?

Fundamentally, the road map content was summarized in aspects as the commitment that had to assume the Palestinian representatives to put an end to terrorism, to write and adopt a Palestinian Constitution, jointly find a solution to the issue of refugees and East Jerusalem, to define the borders and the problem of the settlements. These last points were suggested that they would be discussed later, i.e., this plan had the same format of all previous plans of past summits in the sense that the crucial points, always were of constant postponement. In the road map refers that Israel agrees to freeze the construction of more settlements in the West Bank, but the content of this plan is not enough because the fundamental point in this case is not to freeze Jewish settlements, since Israel must assume a commitment which goes further, as the dismantling of all of them, In this sense, the Zionist State should not pretend to redress the continuous violations of international law, postponing its willingness to follow building more settlements in the West Bank. Indeed, the Israeli attitude was full of hesitation, avoiding a reasonable solution in relation to the future of these settlements.

In this road map is considered that Palestinian demonstrations shown in the year 2000, known by the name of Intifada, are demonstrations that generate violence. But basically the spirit of this widespread protest had the aim to show the world, the Israeli racist system against the Palestinian people that since long time ago the authorities of the occupying forces have been applying. Therefore, many countries do not share the point mentioned in the "road map" related with the intifada, since the history has shown that it is just normal that people who feel oppressed by any form of hostile occupation, have the right to reject it.

In the road map refers to a phase where they have to define provisional borders for a future Palestinian State, but at this point it is impossible to build trust for the simple reason that after more than 20 years of negotiations between Palestinians and Israelis, it is absurd to establish "provisional borders". I am convinced the content of this plan generates serious suspicions, since its intention is to expand the peace process in order to favor Israel and is evidently the lack of clarity in specifying the background of the plan.

Although "the road" map plan envisaged that the most difficult issues as East of Jerusalem, the layout of the final borders, Palestinian refugees and Jewish settlements, were not going to be easy to resolve. But the strange thing of all that, is the fact that always the most important issues that affect directly the Palestinian people, were postponed and this has been happening for over 20 years since the first summit. Is it coincidence? I refuse to believe that it's simply coincidence; rather it is a clear proof that the Americans try to impose a solution that ends up harming the Palestinians and favoring Israel. That is evidenced in the sense that after many years of dialogue, there has been very little progress, especially with the most important points and while that equation is maintained so, we cannot speak of a definitive solution to the conflict.

Several years later, U.S. President George Bush organized a meeting with many guests and representatives of several countries at the end of 2007. That meeting was called the Annapolis Conference. Honoring truth, the advertising framework and expectations that American politicians had created around this Summit, it was far beyond any agreement reached. The two main guests were Israeli Prime Minister Ehud Olmert and the President of the Palestinian national authority, Mahmud Abbas. The commitment that took those two leaders was to redouble their efforts to achieve a peace agreement that ensures an independent Palestinian State, based on the principles of the road map. A few days after this meeting, Israel announced the construction of more settlements in the occupied territories. It was evidenced that the double standards of the Zionist State always remained in all peace talks with the Palestinians.

The last formal meeting between Palestinian and Israeli leaders, it carried out through the intermediary of U.S. President Barak Obama. In a climate in which predominated the distrust and uncertainty, Benjamin Netanyahu and Mahmud Abbas had an appointment in Jerusalem, with the presence of the American Secretary of State Hillary Clinton in September of 2010. The beginning of these contacts could not be worse since Netanyahu told Abbas the intention of Israel to continue with its policy of building more settlements and the expansion of many of the existing settlements in the occupied territories. In this last case, Israel seeks to legitimate them because, according to its interpretation, it is "demographic and natural growth of the settlements". With this "special commencement" was received the Palestinian leader and is needless to say what was the reaction of Abbas towards the cynical, insulting and offensive posture by the Israeli Prime Minister. By simple logic, the meeting ended with a total absence of success.

In view of the endless and constantly Israeli sneer, reflected in its lack of seriousness and determination in the peace dialogues, Mahmud Abbas had thought enough on the topic and came to the conclusion that an impasse had been reached after more than 20 years of meetings with top Israeli leaders, and the so long-awaited self-determination and independence of the Palestinians, was far from to be accomplished and therefore, the Palestinians did not find other different choice than to present a formal request to the United Nations General Assembly, accepting Palestine as an observer State and not as permanent Member, since the Palestinian leader had tried that full recognition as any other State but the test had failed in the UN for lack of consensus. This time the Palestinians wanted to make something that could represent the prelude of an independent State. It should be noted that its approval may be accompanied by ample opportunities because of in the General Assembly is not allowed the use of the veto as has occurred in the UN Security Council. Prior to this important meeting at the UN, Israeli Prime Minister Netanyahu proposed the resumption of the dialogue with the Palestinians "without conditions" to unlock the peace process, but his image, plagued of farces and deception, found not any answer.

In November 2012, the General Assembly of the United Nations met to begin the vote about the Palestinian request and that petition was approved by an overwhelming majority of 138 votes in favor and 9 votes against. Palestine was accepted as a non-member Observer State of the UN, at the same time, Israel said that such a measure was going to hinder any effort to find a solution to the conflict. Immediately, Israeli Prime Minister Netanyahu reported a statement in which said that Israel will continue with its policy of building Jewish settlements in East

Jerusalem and the West Bank.

Photo 7 Source AFP. "At the beginning of August of 2013, were resumed the peace talks between Israeli and Palestinian representatives, through the intermediary of the United States. As in all previous meetings; many handshakes and smiles"

What does mean for Palestinians that the UN has accepted Palestine as a non-member observer State? First, that Resolution supports the legitimate right of the Palestinian people in its aspiration to a Palestinian State under the green line established in 1949, about Resolutions of the United Nations. Abbas had said before the vote was started that it is a moral and historical duty that UN support the creation of a Palestinian State, because 65 years ago this same body had approved the establishment of Israel. In this order of context, the fact that Palestine is part of the UN, means basically that the Palestinian representatives are empowered to take part in the debates of the General Assembly. Moreover, will have access to a body subordinated to the UN as the ICC (International Criminal Court) in The Hague where the

By Kassem Asmar Castellanos

Palestinians may exert the right to present claims that believe necessary against Israel.

To be honest, those were the reasons that Israel wanted to prevent that Palestine was accepted in the UN. Before the vote, Abbas had clarified that the request of the Palestinian people is the central objective and it is subordinated to the achievement of a just peace and the best guarantor and mediator is the United Nations. Most of the United Nations representatives applauded excitedly the words of the Palestinian leader.

The conclusion that can be observed after examining each of these summits and whose discussions aimed to find an Israeli-Palestinian peace agreement but unfortunately have finished in a clear failure, has two permanent components as reasons; the lack of political will and serious commitment by Israel and the prolonged cover-up that leaders of the U.S. Governments have shown with the deceptive tactics of Israel. The world has begun to take note that Israel intends to reach a peace agreement but at the same time seize the occupied territories and precisely these are proposals that make that the Palestinians do not have another option than to continue rejecting them, regardless of how many meetings and summits it will continue organizing.

The question that many people in different parts of the world wonder is: who is right and who is wrong? The truth is that the oppressors can lie, however cannot change registers and records of historical and contemporary events as they used to do a few decades ago, because the information today is within the reach of everyone. Palestinian people don't lose the hope of seeing through windows and doors in the occupied territories, a picture free of settlements and Zionist soldiers. I want to conclude this work with a famous phrase written more than 150 years ago:

"Those who deny freedom to others do not deserve it for themselves; because under a just God they can't keep it for a long time".

Abraham Lincoln

By Kassem Asmar Castellanos

BIBLIOGRAPHY

PAPPÉ Ilan. The Ethnic cleansing of Palestine. Editorial review

PAPPÉ Ilan. History of modern Palestine, a land two peoples. Editorial Akal SHLAIM Avi. The wall of iron, Israel and the Arab world. Publishing Almed SAND Shlomo. The invention of the Jewish people. Editorial Akal

Norman FINKELSTEIN. The Holocaust industry. Publishing century XXI

Norman FINKELSTEIN. Image and reality of the Israel-Palestine conflict. Editorial Akal Jimmy CARTER. Palestine: peace and not Apartheid. Publisher Simon & Schuster CHOMSKY Noam. Gaza in crisis. Taurus publishing

MORRIS Benny. The birth of the Palestinian refugee problem.

Nurit Peled-Elhanan. Palestinian school textbooks; ideology and propaganda in education